BASED ON A TRUE STORY

Three Strokes in Three Weeks
Saved My Life

A Journey Toward Finding Oneself

Leo Costa Jr.

PAGE PUBLISHING, INC.
New York, NY

First originally published by Page Publishing, Inc. 2016

ISBN 978-1-63417-667-5 (pbk)
ISBN 978-1-63417-668-2 (digital)

Printed in the United States of America

CONTENTS

PROLOGUE

All the world's a stage, and all the men and women merely players; They have their exits and their entrances; and one man in his time plays many parts, his acts being seven ages.

— William Shakespeare, As You Like It

Sweat dripped from under my baseball cap and rolled down the sides of my face as I pulled back on the overhead lat bar. I weighed 300 pounds and was trying to lift 200 pounds. "Ready? Go," urged Tom Platz, my spotter, as he pushed down hard on the bar. I caught the downward momentum and leaned back until I was nearly horizontal on the bench. I grunted through the pain that felt like walking into a fire. At the time, in January 2011, I was living my life at very extreme levels as I trained to compete in a national bodybuilding competition. I suffered every single workout, but it didn't matter. It only mattered that I ended up on stage.

William Shakespeare hit the nail on the head. My life has definitely unfolded across several acts on a world stage, and I have played many parts. Sometimes life is like a movie, an old country song, and even a famous quote. Now that I am 59 years old, I have the tremendous advantage of having experienced quite a bit in life. My father always told me it's very difficult to replace experience.

More than ever, I think he is right. No doubt there's something to be said in having firsthand experience as opposed to having learned something through someone else's trial and error or perhaps out of a book. Not to say that the latter two are not useful because they are. However, when we live the experience firsthand we're able to understand it on a more personal level and appreciate its own unique perspective. We all have a life story that can be told or even examined, each one being unique to us and yet so similar to others.

We are all the same but different, you might say. We experience good times and bad. We will feel happiness, heartache, frustration, and anger. We will have moments, events, and experiences that define us and help develop the color of our life. These times will guide us through those side streets, detours, roads, and freeways, taking us on our personal journey from cradle to coffin.

In the story that follows, I am using myself and my experiences as a means to motivate, educate, and empower others. I want to motivate people to change their mind-sets from just settling to reaching for their ultimate potential. I want to educate people using my own experiences and training background from sports and bodybuilding. I want to empower people to be proactive about their health and recovery. I want to give people the tools to overcome adversity and achieve success.

The past, present, and future are the main components that can serve as the framework of our life. In other words, they offer a foundation from which we can chart our own unique path. I think life becomes more meaningful when we are lucky enough to be able to look back. The past (*Hindsight*) can be a valuable tool to evaluate, learn, and move forward. However, as in many cases, looking back too long, dwelling upon something beyond absurdity can be stifling. There is always the present (*Now*), which in my opinion is the most important because it gives us the opportunity to live in real time and in the moments.

When we are aware and living in the moment, we can be the captain of our ship. Living in the present allows us to make life's game-time decisions in the everyday occurrences and events of our lives. This is where we can possibly create our own destiny, by the reflection of our own lives as well as the potential of what's to come. All because of the decisions we make to act, to react, or to pass on.

Thinking about the future (*Imaginary*), is an interesting concept. If we believe that what we think about can affect the outcome of our future, then being in this state of mind creates an opportunity for us to dream. This is difficult for some people and yet for others like myself, is a part of normal everyday existence and helps us to envision our future.

So here is a question to ponder. How can we possibly gain more control over our lives? Should we bother to try when it seems even with the best-laid plans, life rarely cooperates? It's like trying to predict the weather. It's pretty tricky, and yet we have meteorologists who attempt this daily.

Even though there are many factors that can cause unforeseen surprises and outcomes, there are also trends and repeated behavior that can be predictable. Based on this undeniable fact, I think we should give it a college try. To me it makes sense in the same way it does to have the advantage of a map guiding us to our destination versus having no map at all. It minimizes the chance of getting lost, but it doesn't guarantee that we won't.

This life is OUR road map, and our age determines how vast our map is. We have the ability to navigate, learn, solve problems, minimize mistakes, make history, and choose the color of our life.

As I'm writing this and reflecting on my life, I've come to an understanding. There are things that have happened. They have had a profound effect on me to an extent that caused a shift in how I think and act. I also believe that in order for this shift to have happened, something had to have impacted me at the deepest level. It got my undivided attention, and potentially almost took my life.

A picture of me at one of my photo shoots after winning Mr. USA Mens Nationals (heavy weight division) in Las Vegas, California.

CHAPTER ONE

The Paradigm Shift

From life's school of war: what does not kill me makes me stronger.

— Friedrich Nietzche

January 27, 2011, was just another ordinary day for me. I had hit 30 years of owning my own personal training business, which was something I enjoyed doing every day. I worked in my studio gym helping clients get in their best shape; I liked being a part of their life-changing transformation. Who wouldn't enjoy this? In addition, I was also continuing to move forward as a competitive athlete in the sport of bodybuilding. All of this had become a hobby, a passion, and my life's work.

I had just come out of retirement from bodybuilding after a 13-year break. I was excited to try it again at the age of 53, just to see what it would feel like. I was in my third year of getting ready to compete in the men's nationals in the master division, which was the biggest amateur event one could compete in before turning pro. That was my goal. The event would be held in late July of that year in Pittsburgh, Pennsylvania. Leading up to the nationals, I was competing at smaller events to see if in fact I could get myself back to my best condition when I had competed in my forties. I knew it would be a tall order, but I always loved a difficult challenge.

Remarkably, after two years and my first two competitions back from retirement, I was able to get pretty close to my all-time best condition. I was very confident that with one more year of intense training, I could do it. Turning pro would mean that my childhood dream had finally come true.

By that January I was about six months from being competition ready for the biggest event of my bodybuilding career. My training was as intense as ever, and I was enjoying every moment it took to get on stage. It was so addicting and all consuming. Even when I was training for a competition, I continued to train clients. They were always interested and amazed to watch my transformation. One evening as I was finishing up with a client, I experienced a very strange occurrence, one that had never happened before.

I had my right leg propped up on the workout bench, leaning on it as I observed my client, when all of a sudden a jolt came through my body. As I slowly took my foot off the bench, I knew something was wrong. I couldn't find the ground with my foot. I felt somewhat disconnected in this moment from my body. Within minutes, when I went to put my hand on the workout bench to sit down, I couldn't make my hand go where I wanted it to. I could feel my body losing the ability to function properly, and my instincts told me I was in trouble.

Like a wave rolling through my body, much like a domino effect, I noticed I was now having trouble talking and felt somewhat disoriented. My body was under attack, but I didn't have a clue as to what was happening to me. I had been hurt many times earlier in my athletic career playing football and was prone to concussions. It was oddly similar to how I felt at this moment, but I knew this was something different. The disorientation felt familiar, but I was also rapidly losing all of my motor function. I tried to regroup, but I just couldn't.

Now all I wanted more than anything was to be at home, which was about a 15-minute drive from the gym. I was apprehensive, but I grabbed my keys anyway and got in my truck. As I was driving, I could feel my body losing more function. My vision became impaired. I remember being about two minutes from home and not knowing if I was going to make it. At that point, I was driving ever so slowly to avoid having an accident.

Amazingly, I was able to park my car in the garage and stumble into my house where I suddenly crashed into the wall. My wife Tina rushed to my side and dragged me over to a chair. I'll never forget the terrified look in her eyes. In that moment I felt so bad for her: I could see her fear. As much trouble as I knew I was in, I wasn't scared. She wanted to call an ambulance, but I refused. I didn't know what was happening to me, but years of competitive athletic experience told me I could beat it.

This is exactly how I responded when I had gotten injured years earlier playing football. I never wanted to go to the doctor, or give in, because I thought I could tough it out. I was stubborn, but fortunately my wife called Shane, my oldest son, to come to the house. They ended up calling the ambulance, and I'm lucky they did. Once I got to Kaweah Delta Hospital, the intake doctors and nurses quickly determined I had a stroke. Not long after I was admitted to the emergency room, I had another.

I was now paralyzed on my right side from head to toe, with my arm and hand being the most impaired. If my family hadn't called the ambulance when they did, the outcome might have been very different. From one day to the next, I went from being in complete control of my mind and body to being paralyzed on the right side from head to toe, not knowing how to move my arm or even understanding where it was in space. It was as if I was completely disconnected from the right side of my body.

When a medical event like this happens, you undergo a variety of extensive tests for your heart, brain, and the rest of your vitals, all for the sole purpose of finding out why the stroke happened in the first place and to prevent subsequent events. Unbelievably, after all the testing was done, the doctor's results stunned me. No heart damage. No cholesterol issues. No blockage of the carotid arteries. My blood pressure was slightly elevated but not out of the normal range.

The doc said I shouldn't be in the hospital and yet, here I was. He could find no conclusive evidence for why this had happened to me. This was good news and bad news. The best explanation for the strokes was the dangerous combination of stress, sleep deprivation, and extreme training that I was undergoing for the upcoming bodybuilding competition.

When the first two strokes hit me, I was lucky enough to get to the hospital in time to take advantage of a stroke treatment called Tissue Plasminogen Activator (TPA), which quickly dissolves blood clots. This treatment is considered somewhat controversial because of the risk of potential death due to the individual bleeding out. However, if it works within two to three days post treatment, it can eliminate any indication that a stroke ever occurred. I motioned to Josh, my younger son, to sign the consent form. I was willing to take the chance because I wasn't willing to live like that.

It was amazing. I had two strokes on a Thursday that paralyzed my speech, right arm, hand, and leg, but by Sunday I could walk out of the hospital as if the strokes had never happened. The doctor told me I should take at least a month off, if not six weeks, to rest and recover. I knew what the doctor suggested was for my own good; however, I thought four to six weeks was too long. Maybe I should have listened, but I didn't. He strongly advised me not to compete in the sport of bodybuilding because of the inherent danger of pushing one's body to its limits. I was disappointed beyond belief hearing my doctor tell me to take time off.

I made it quite clear to him I would follow his orders and retire from the sport of bodybuilding, something I really loved doing. I knew down deep that if I kept bodybuilding for competition it might kill me and yet while I was at home recovering, the thought of competing again was all I could think about.

Three days after my first two strokes, I decided to go back to the gym. Even though this was not what the doctor ordered, I rationalized that I felt fine, and I would not go back to bodybuilding; however, I would start a modified exercise routine specifically for health and fitness.

As far as my work schedule was concerned, it would be limited to a few hours a day. I really thought the doctor's recommendations were meant for the average person who was more out of shape and not an athlete. I just wanted to get my life back to normal—with some new adjustments—and move on. So I tried. I eased my way back, monitoring myself, and I seemed fine.

Three weeks to the day from my first two strokes, lightning struck again. I could feel it coming and immediately stopped training my clients and drove myself straight to the hospital. I pulled up to the ER, walked up to the front desk, and told them I was having a stroke. They took me to the back room to fill out some paperwork and all of a sudden I crashed. I was once again impaired on the right side of my body just as before.

The major difference between this third stroke and my first two was the fact that now I did not have the option of getting the TPA treatment. Not enough time had passed since the first two strokes. This meant that I would have to deal with my paralysis and recovery with every ounce of energy and desire and all the unwavering bulldog attitude I could muster.

Over the next few days, my mental state became more objective. I was now searching my mind for answers that would lead me on a personal fact-finding mission. I decided to use hindsight and analyze my life as a spectator, from the beginning. I wanted to see if there was anything I could have done differently that might have changed history, and to learn more about myself and my challenges beforehand, hoping that my life, up to this point, would be able to help me overcome this. Here's what I discovered.

Phase One

Birth to Twenty-One Years Old

CHAPTER TWO

A Young Obsession

If it's important to you, you will find a way. If not, you'll find an excuse.

—Frank Banks

My first real recollection of being aware that I was among the living was when I was four years old, and I was in a crib in my mom and dad's bedroom. I was awakened by my mom, who had gone into early labor with my sister, Leanne. Otherwise, up to this point, I had no idea I was alive. Until the age of six, the only other thing I really remember about my life was that my mom and dad were divorcing. My mom left with my sister and me, and we moved out of Visalia, California, to my aunt's house in Hanford, about 20 minutes away. I remember being confused. I missed having my dad around and had to learn how to adjust to the divorce.

Divorce is definitely trying for all involved. Looking back now, it wasn't the worst thing in the world that could have happened, but at times it felt like it. We don't get out of this life without getting bruised, if not worse. Life is going to test us whether we like it or not.

Old sayings always seem to have a ring of truth to them. In the last year and a half especially I can relate to "You don't know what you have until it's gone" and "What does not kill me makes me stronger." But I was already learning about some of these sayings during my childhood.

Except for having fun playing with my cousins, my early life kind of sucked. Looking back, I realize that I lived my life in phases of extreme behavior. I can remember this beginning when I was around six or seven years old. Living like this has its benefits and drawbacks, and as life usually does, it taught me the benefit of both.

Even though I wasn't fully aware at the time, I first experienced extreme behavior when I started playing sports. I loved sports and was immediately hooked. Sports allowed me to fantasize and dream, which made me feel amazing. They were a good distraction, which helped me deal with what was going on in my personal life. My mom was a single working parent, which meant there were times I didn't have as much supervision as necessary. Before I was introduced to sports, I had begun rebelling and acting out. Hindsight being the valuable tool that it is, I now realize that I was definitely doing this as a result of my parents' divorce.

I remember walking to school, which was about three blocks away from my house. I hated going to my new school, so at times I would ditch. Instead, I would hang out around the neighborhood playing marbles by myself, just waiting for my little buddies to get out of school so I could play them. A lot of my friends and I were collectors and had become very competitive when it came to playing each other. We had no money to bet; however, we had marbles.

I got really good at this game and made it a point to beat my buddies, which really helped add to my growing collection. Playing marbles, especially against my friends, became addictive. I now remember how obsessed I was about winning and becoming a connoisseur of marbles. My favorites were small cat's-eye marbles, which came in a variety of spectacular colors, and small steely, or metal, marbles. This was just one of the many things I did back then with my friends.

I also remember playing with fireworks, smoking my mom's cigarettes on top of the garage, and going to the local supermarket just down the street to steal the little prizes out of the cereal boxes. My little friends and I would work together as a team to pull this off successfully. One of us would be the lookout while the other would be the thief. I was getting into some potentially dangerous mischief, but luckily this is when I was introduced to sports.

My dad had decided to take me to a local junior college football game one Saturday night, and that's where I found my passion for life. The thing that stuck with me most from the games was the half-time events. Before the team came back out, the fans went down on the field and made a tunnel for the players to run through. When those players ran by, they looked bigger than life itself and seemed like gods to me. It was such an adrenaline rush. That feeling would stay with me for days after the games were over.

I remember I couldn't wait for Monday's newspaper so I could look at the sports section to see if there were any action photos of the game. I would cut them out and add them to the new scrapbook that I had started. They were a perfect distraction to the disarray in my personal life. I would stare at those photos for hours, dreaming about the day when I would be in those very pictures, in my own action shots. As it turned out, it happened a lot throughout my sports career.

As I'm writing this now, I'm more than a bit shocked at some of the mischievous behavior I got into at such a young age. Now I understand that my actions had a lot to do with the insecurity of being in the middle of a badly handled divorce. Fortunately, I didn't turn into a hardened criminal at the age of six and somehow managed to make it to second grade.

But there was more change coming my way. My mom decided to move again. I would be attending another new school the following year. In a way I was actually glad about this because even though I had made some friends, the thought of going back to the same school where I hated first grade gave me a really bad feeling.

At seven years old, I was already pretty well traveled. I went from living on a family dairy farm in Visalia to moving into town and attending three different schools. Our past can be so telling about how we respond in the present as well as our ability to dream about the future. Now that I'm older and able to reflect on my past, I've learned that I had good survival skills, which was obvious even at a young age. I learned to adapt to frequent moves, going to new schools, and dealing with being caught between divorced parents.

Second grade brought more self-discovery. I learned that I was really good at every sport I played. I especially loved football, basketball, and baseball. I really seemed to like all three the same. They kept me really busy after school all year round, which kept me from getting into mischief. I also seemed to like second grade way better than first. Even though the divorce between my parents was still somewhat contentious, I found myself adapting and moving forward. As different sports became a bigger part of my life, they offered a good distraction to my personal problems.

Another distraction was a girl named Janet. She sat right in front of me in class. She was really cute and as the school year went on, I developed my first crush. What is now evident is that the things I was most interested in became my obsessions. Cleary that was the case with sports, and it seemed as if my little girl crush was also falling into that category.

During this time, we had a babysitter named Ethel Spitig. Now, let me explain something. Ethel was no ordinary babysitter. In fact, she was exactly what every kid didn't want. I'm not exaggerating the truth when I say this woman was the worst part of my day. When dinner came around she would make food that my sister and I didn't like, and I'm pretty sure she did it on purpose. She would make us sit next to one another at the dinner table while she sat facing us. Her goal was to make sure we ate all the food on our plates, while our goal was to get away from that table as fast as we could. We would try to trick her by hiding food under our tongues or feeding it to our dog when she wasn't looking. The funny thing is that we didn't like the food, but our dog sure did. Maybe she should have made the food for him instead. Dinnertime was such a traumatic experience. It was a nightmare that I was living every day. We complained so much about her to our mother that eventually she let her go, which was the best thing that could have happened.

Around this time in my life I also started really enjoying flag football. I loved it. I was now starting to play out on a field, something I had been dreaming and fantasizing about for the last year. What I remember the most about flag football was being able to fake people out with my moves and scoring a lot of touchdowns. I really enjoyed when the fans on the sideline would cheer me on while I was running down the field. It made me run even faster and gave me such a rush.

It seemed so natural to do what I was doing on the field. I was just reacting and it was as if my body knew where it was going before my mind did. Little did I know, at the age of eight, what kind of impact sports would have on my life and how this kind of adulation would become addictive. From this point forward sports became a staple in my life and my safe haven. It was where I felt the most comfortable, and it gave me a sense of security. With all the divorce drama that was going on, that was exactly what I needed.

An old friend and I hanging out
during little league practice at the age of 9.

By the time I was in the eighth grade, I was heavily involved in sports. It was definitely the center of my life. I played sports all year-round. I was a three-sport athlete playing football, basketball, and baseball. I was always voted captain of the team and seemed to be the leader whose play on the field set the example for how we played as a team. I was learning so many life lessons at an early age, and I didn't even know it. All I knew was that I was in my zone.

One of the things athletics teaches us is how to deal with adversity in order to achieve greatness. If we play team sports, we must learn how to compete against, coexist alongside, and play with our own team-mates. It's an interesting dynamic when we're trying to beat out our buddy for a starting position. We're either supported or resented.

Eventually as we continue playing and competing more, we learn about ourselves and what we're made of. Sports will test us. We continuously have to figure ways to succeed throughout all the highs and lows. I've never felt so much euphoria as I have from winning in sports, and yet the losses could be so much more devastating. The wins never felt as good as the losses stung.

Life is similar to athletics. Sometimes things go well, even great, and sometimes they go horribly wrong. Everything seems out of sync, and we find ourselves in a horrible slump. When this happens, and it's not if but when, be prepared for it to happen again and again. Learn how to overcome it and take the positive from it. In sports, as in life, we have to live in the present moments; however, we should look back in hindsight as a reference, to be able to deal with what's coming next.

We must learn that success is fleeting and will come in moments, and we probably won't learn much beyond the win. However, those times should be enjoyed. Adversity is the real teacher, leading to more successes. If we can wrap our thoughts around this notion, then we're on to something big. It's not an easy task because we're constantly dealing with failure, and it takes a boatload of failure before we really get good at anything challenging.

One of the things that gave me success throughout my sports career was being able to do the work necessary on a daily basis. I pushed my body and mind to prepare myself for what was going to come my way throughout my athletic future, continuously being challenged to do what is required in order to succeed at something. Some of us will take the easy road that requires less effort and settle, while others choose to do the work necessary. Why do we sometimes doubt the potential we have? I would later learn more about this, but right then, sports were becoming the most important thing in my life.

They were all I could think about. I ate, drank, and slept sports. I would practice for hours, all the while creating scenarios and visualizing myself in game-time situations. I would imagine exactly how I would perform on the field. It felt so real. From seventh grade through my freshman year in high school, sports came naturally to me. I picked up on things quickly and had a good IQ for each sport I was in. And in this short period of time, I was experiencing way more success than failure.

I hadn't suffered any kind of setbacks like injuries other than a twisted ankle here and there. My mind and body were in sync, and things were going great in my life and sports world. I didn't know it, but I was about to learn some life lessons in the upcoming year. It was now my sophomore year in high school. Two-a-day practices for football had begun. I would be trying to earn a starting position on the junior varsity team as a quarterback. The main reason I chose the quarterback position was that I would be involved in every play on offense.

It was also a position that required a varied skill set more than any other position on the team. You needed to be able to run with the ball when necessary and throw the ball with accuracy, and you had to know what every other player's responsibility was on the offensive side of the football. Over time I learned that how I chose to think potentially affected my energy and attitude. This had a significant impact on how the rest of the players on offense behaved and even how the team played as a whole. I see now how this became a life lesson, presenting itself time and time again as I journeyed through life and sports.

It all starts in our minds. Thought is the most powerful thing that humans possess, and yet we use only a fraction of what we have. Essentially the ongoing daily challenge is to engage our minds in various instances, learning how to be proactive, reactive, and productive. Sometimes we have to do this in a split second, and sometimes over long grueling periods of time.

Learning and becoming the master of our life and our life's work is a marathon, not a sprint. Sports were and continue to be the platform that gives me the opportunities to learn about life and myself at the deepest level. One thing I've learned is that we're more resilient than we think. I would experience this both on the stage of life and in the arena of sports.

CHAPTER THREE

Believe in Yourself

Never give in, never give in, never, never, never, never....

—Winston Churchill

Unlike my first experience in sports at eight years old and all the way through my freshman year in high school, my sophomore year was like rediscovering myself all over again. I began to notice that something was different about the way my mind and body were synced up. Actually, it was more like out of sync. It was the beginning of football season in my sophomore year. I was very excited, even though I would be playing on the junior varsity team. The players who were going to play junior varsity would, for about two to three weeks, practice with the varsity coaches and players before we split up into our own teams.

The fact that I was a sophomore able to practice with and around some of the older players was not only exciting but also a very good learning experience. You could really see the separation between me and the varsity guys, in terms of experience and the overall speed at which they did their drills.

It was eye opening and a bit intimidating for me, a young player, but at the same time a good, up-close look and a measuring stick as to what I had to do in order to play at the varsity level. From my freshman year to my sophomore year, I had a bit of a growth spurt. Somehow, as I discovered, this affected my feet. Unlike when I was eight years old, my body was not responding and reacting on the field in the way I was used to it doing.

In fact, it was as if I didn't even know where my feet were in space. All of a sudden I was a bit clumsy, if not a lot, with my foot work. I noticed this in drills I had to do as a part of improving my skills at the quarterback position. It was odd and frustrating to experience this disconnect between my mind and body. I did not like it. In my sophomore year of football I experienced a combination of some success but a whole lot more frustration because I never felt like my mind and body ever synced up as one.

In addition, I had my first injury, which kept me on the sidelines for a couple of weeks and was absolute torture. I felt helpless. I was the first-string quarterback, and being the quarterback on the football team meant being a leader of the team. Because of the high profile nature of the position, the quarterback typically gets a lot of attention: good, bad, deserved, and undeserved.

Quarterbacks are considered heroes or goats depending on whether or not the team's winning or losing is being blamed on them. Strangely, this was one of the things that attracted me to the position. I've always liked difficult if not seemingly impossible challenges.

The second-string quarterback who took over while I was injured was playing very well. In fact, his play sparked the team. Another life lesson was about to come knocking on my door. The longer you play sports, the more things will happen, good and bad. It always seemed to be true.

There were at least three or four times during my high school and college days as an athlete that I was either injured or benched because of a lack of productive play on the field. Without fail, the athlete who replaced me would come in and play well and invariably spark team play in a positive way. Too positive, as far as I was concerned.

Coaches, for the most part, are motivated and defined by wins and losses. Athletes are defined by their productive play, which reflects the coach's "what have you done lately" mentality. In a nutshell, it means that you better play well pretty consistently or face the consequences of being benched. Inevitably at some time during an athlete's career, he will get benched. This is an ugly reality and part of the game, and the athlete has to learn to deal with it.

Typically when you are replaced due to an injury, it is not the same as when you get benched due to poor performance on the field. This is an unwritten rule. From the athletes' perspective, this always feels somewhat reassuring; however, the reality of this can never really be counted on simply because of the inherent pressure that's put on coaches to win.

This scenario creates a potential recipe for disaster and added pressure. The athlete is always faced with uncertainty about the security of getting back his starting position. In addition, when the second-stringer is doing well, all of a sudden he starts gaining the support of the team, which is normal. But to the injured athlete who feels helpless on the sidelines, paranoia, fear, and doubt begin to creep into the psyche.

I was about to learn my first life lesson. It was "believe in yourself." Throughout athletics and in life there will be times of adversity when it all sucks beyond belief. We are always being tested, and because I had started sports at such an early age, I believe I learned some life lessons on the field before I first experienced them in life.

As I got older, there were no shortages of life lessons. I was being challenged over and over again. This taught me all about adversity, failure, defeat, and success. Reflecting back, I realize that learning how to truly believe in yourself is one of the best life lessons you can ever learn. There have been many times throughout my life as well as in my sports career when I really had to believe in my capabilities even when very few did.

I remember vividly the feelings I felt during these times of adversity. It was gut-wrenching. Life sucked. My stomach would be in knots, and it seemed like time slowed to a painful crawl. All I wanted was for things to go back to normal so I could feel good again. But being injured and experiencing those feelings of doubt, in the scope of things, made me mentally stronger and a better athlete.

As much as I hated the experiences, those times on the sidelines gave me a chance to do a lot of thinking and soul searching. I eventually figured out I could make myself proactive and productive, which went against everything I was feeling. When you're as competitive as I am, watching from the sidelines is not an option, but at times it is a hard reality.

Sometimes in life we are faced with challenges. We may feel lost, confused, or scared, but adversity can do one of two things: it can either destroy us or define us.

I reluctantly made that choice. When we want something bad enough, we have to be willing to do the work, no matter what distracting obstacles come our way. I was going to do whatever it took to be better and succeed. Instead of focusing on being on the sidelines, angry at my coach, hoping my competition would screw up, and letting my own self-doubt and insecurity get the best of me, I decided to focus on things I could do to be proactive, so that when I did get back to playing again, I would be a better athlete with more skills and a stronger mentality.

One thing I did while watching from the sidelines was to study and observe the game from the perspective of a coach, as opposed to a player. For example, I would pay attention to how the opponent was defending the plays our coaches were calling, how we executed those plays, and the result.

This strategy in the long run would serve me well in a positive way because sooner or later I would get another chance on the field to prove myself. The fact I chose to be proactive and productive increased my chances of being more successful on the playing field. Life at times can be intense. It's an express ride and will go on with or without you. You either take the ride of life or sit on its sidelines and watch it go by.

Things eventually worked out for me. I got back my starting position. History would end up repeating itself throughout my athletic career as it often does in life. I dealt with injuries, being benched, and difficult coaches, but I continued to move forward, learning from my mistakes and challenges, making them work for me and not against me.

Tough Running

It takes two Delano tacklers to bring down Mt. Whitney quarterback Leo Costa after Costa picked up some yardage against the Tigers Friday night in the Mineral King Bowl.
— Times-Delta Photo

Article from way back in the day when I was the Mt. Whitney quarterback. Here I am getting tackled in a high school football game. This article is from the local newspaper Times Delta.

As in athletics and in the game of life, the chance of getting another shot to redeem ourselves will happen, so why not believe in ourselves? It's good practice and it takes a lot of it. Easier said than done.

History teaches us things, so being able to reflect is a powerful tool to develop a strategy and a course of action. So many times, as in my example, we are not aware of what we are really going through and how our physiology is being directed by our mind through its own built-in intuition, creating tools for us to be able to adapt to a variety of situations.

This is what's known as "fight or flight" response, which is our body's primitive, automatic, inborn response that prepares it to fight or flee from perceived attack, harm, or threat to our survival. As a 14-year-old sophomore in high school, I was facing adversity through sports. Little did I know that my body was trying to take care of me, as well as helping me to develop tools and skills that would be extremely useful and responsible for my ongoing development as the person I would eventually become. I was clueless!

CHAPTER FOUR

Work Ethic

Listen to your inner voice; it's your guiding light.

—Leo Costa, Jr.

Even though I was a multiple-sport athlete, my favorite sport became football. I loved the contact and the challenge of playing quarterback. Before I knew it, the summer before my junior year in high school had arrived. All I could think about was football and playing on the varsity team.

Sports had become my passionate addiction and the center of my universe. I wanted to keep improving my skills. I didn't know how much work it would take, and how far I could push my body. I worked hard during the summer getting ready for a much-anticipated football season. I could feel my body changing. Unlike the previous year, I started noticing I had more control over my body, especially my feet, and I had grown a couple of inches. Once again two-a-day football, otherwise known as hell week, had begun.

This would be my third year of playing tackle football and my seventh year of playing at the quarterback position. By this time playing with all of the equipment, specifically the helmet and pads, had become more natural. I was now fully aware that I would be looked upon as one of the leaders of the varsity team. I was ready. I wanted to lead by example and felt confident going into the season as I had worked hard over the summer to be prepared.

During my junior year I learned that as hard as I pushed my mind and body, I never saw it as work, and yet it really was. I learned the more I worked at perfecting my craft, the luckier I got. As a junior in high school, playing varsity football, I had no idea what a work ethic really was, but what I did know was that I was totally consumed by football. I would later learn that having a passion for what I did would play a major role in determining which path I would follow throughout my life. My junior year ended up being a pivotal year with respect to personal growth and reaching new levels of standout play on the field.

I had some disappointing moments, though, with regard to some injuries. I was hurt early in the season with a separated shoulder, and I missed two games. Then I missed the last game of the year, our big, crosstown rivalry game, due to a broken arm. But this never stopped me. One of the highlights of my junior season was the improved leadership skills I developed.

I pushed myself every day on the practice field, and I felt that by leading by example, I had a positive influence on my teammates. Not only did I get more out of my abilities, but so did the players around me. It was about developing good habits through good practice, otherwise known as repetitions. I made it a point every practice to arrive early and leave late. Another positive building block from my junior year was that after several years of seasons with a losing record, our team experienced a new trend.

Another thing I was really happy about was that from one year to the next my body seemed like it was again synced up with my brain.

Unlike in my sophomore year, I actually knew where my body was in space. This really gave me more confidence because now I didn't have to think so much about my agility on the field. This allowed me to focus on improving my quarterbacking skills. I began to show flashes of the athlete I wanted to be.

Heading Up Field

Mt. Whitney running back Tom Dancey grabs a pitch out from quarterback Leo Costa and is about to head up field against Delano. Ready to throw a block is Pioneer tackle Steve Parker (66). — Times-Delta Photos by Rock Kendall

Here is another picture that was featured in the local newspaper of me pitching the ball to my running back.

Football had become very good for me. Some critical elements of the game grabbed my attention. It's one of the few sports considered to be truly a team sport. Each and every action performed by the individual athlete on the field has a positive or negative result. It's like a domino effect. Every player, depending on the position he plays, has a specific action to execute. Every individual action is a part of a whole.

I faced some adversity with injuries and at times subpar play, but I tried not to let that get the best of me. To learn how to win in the game of sports, and as I would continue to learn, in the game of life, we must believe in ourselves and have a good work ethic. Through hard work, focus, and perseverance I redeemed myself. Overall I was happy with that, and I felt like I then had developed a foundation from which I could build.

Once again upon reflection, I observe, and I question life more than ever. Not that it makes a difference other than to keep my sense of wonder. Life has a way of constantly testing us, sometimes at the deepest level. It's unclear why at times good and bad things happen, and why some things will never make sense. Like sports, there will be prosperity and adversity, good times and bad. Success is but a fleeting moment: Not much is learned in comparison to the lessons we learn from failure.

CHAPTER FIVE

Be Humble or Get Humbled

To achieve great things you must be willing to fail . . .
Fail hard.

—Leo Costa, Jr.

It's amazing how time flies. Next thing I know, I was starting my senior year and my last season as a high school athlete. Over the summer I started getting letters from universities expressing interest in my abilities. Essentially, I was being scouted as a potential candidate to come play for their schools. There was even the possibility of receiving an athletic scholarship.

WASHINGTON STATE UNIVERSITY

PULLMAN, WASHINGTON 99163 *"Fighting Cougars"*

DEPARTMENT OF INTERCOLLEGIATE ATHLETICS

June, 1972

Dear Prospect:

You have been recommended by your own coach, as well as others in the league, as a top college prospect for next year. As you know Washington State University has one of the best foot-ball programs in the nation and plays in the PACIFIC-8 Confer-ence.

As a Californian you are acquainted with excellent football -- yet should you play at Washington State you would be a distance of a day's drive from your home. Washington State is a super outdoor area, an excellent university, and a top-flight football program.

If you have a sincere interest in going away to school to play in the very best competition, please return the enclosed question-naire so we can begin a file on you. We appreciate your honesty from the start.

Best of luck this season.

Sincerely,

Walt Cubley
Assistant Football Coach
W.S.U. "FIGHTING COUGARS"

WC:ks

One of my recruiting letters that I received during my senior year at Mt. Whitney. This one is from Washington State University, which was one of the best football programs in the nation.

THE PHILLIES
VETERANS STADIUM
BROAD ST. & PATTISON AVE.
PHILADELPHIA, PA. 19148

Dear _Leo_ :

On August 14, 15, and 16, the Philadelphia Phillies
are having a baseball clinic and games in Redding, California.
This will not be a general try-out camp but rather by invitation
only. I am inviting just nine prospects from the Central Valley
area. There will be prospects also from the Bay Area and Northern
California. If you care to go, there should be good competition
and the chance to evaluate yourself with some of the better
players in the State.

We will ride up in station-wagons and stay at the
Ponderosa Motel across from the ballpark. Your meals and lodg-
ing will be taken care of and all arrangements have been approved
by the C.I.F.

Please indicate on the enclosed postcard if you would
like to go. I will then be talking with your parents within the
next several days.

Sincerely,

Ollie Bidwell

Ollie Bidwell
Phillies
Telephone (209) 227-0507

An invitation to go to a training camp for the Philadelphia
Phillies, which is a professional team in Major League Baseball.

I was so excited. The thought of someone thinking I was good enough to get a full-ride scholarship was a huge ego booster. It didn't take long before the kids at school knew. It really made me popular with more than just my teammates. Teachers knew as well as girls, girls, girls, even the kids that didn't play sports. It's kind of weird when strangers know who you are.

My high school senior year in football was a launching pad for the next four years to come. I had broken all kinds of school records. I was on a roll athletically and on a whirlwind express ride. The life lessons of believing in yourself and having an excellent work ethic, which fortunately I had learned by then, were paying big dividends.

The hard work and time spent in preparation to be successful in sports was a testament to what the mind and body could and would endure as long as I was willing to sacrifice and persevere. As a result, I was being offered many full athletic scholarships, attracting notoriety, and becoming very popular. This became extremely addictive, and I loved it. At times I felt like a celebrity with all the press and attention I was getting. What an adrenaline rush. I was hooked and wanted more. Actor Kevin Costner, who became one of my close friends, once told me, "Being famous is intoxicating; however, it can blindside you."

I often have to learn things the hard way, and this time was no different. I decided to stay in town and go to the community college, College of the Sequoias. I was very close to my family, and I had never been away from home. The thought of it frightened me. This was the first difficult decision I made. It might have not been the best one, but at this time in my life, it felt like the right one. The next two years in college were a pretty big transition. With each year, I had to learn how to deal with new challenges, including more freedom and responsibility.

This was just another whole can of worms, which was marked by temptation, and had a life lesson as a kicker. My first year in college was really great, more football, girls, and parties, with some academics thrown in. , we think we're invincible, and because we're young, we're too dumb to know we're not. This was the beginning of when I started, ever so slowly, to abuse my body. It was happening in a few ways. It started with alcohol and the celebration parties after the football games. I celebrated whether we won or lost, so essentially it was a party every weekend. In addition to my alcohol consumption, I started smoking cigarettes. I only smoked them at the after-game parties, so it seemed rather harmless. Yeah, right!

College years were definitely a time of transition, athletically and in my personal life. In sports, even though I had some fantastic highlights, I became increasingly frustrated. Sports had meant everything to me, and I never really thought of anything else I might do.

My first real defining moments happened during this time. They would impact the rest of my life, and would become my foundation and eventually provide me with the resources to take on all of life's challenges and lessons. One defining moment was a football game I played in during my second year of junior college. Our team was highly ranked statewide and had earned a playoff berth in the semifinals. It was such an exciting time in my life and sports career. I had one of the best years ever playing organized football. Getting the opportunity to play in this big game was not only special, but potentially it could advance my sports career.

As with many times in life, things didn't work out as I'd hoped. Losing that game was one of the first bitter disappointments in my sports career. It was devastating because I felt that the reason we lost was because of a decision I had made. You see, I was the quarterback of my team, which is a position that carries a lot of responsibility. It has its perks, but like everything else in life, it also has its downsides. It was the last play of the game, and time was running out. We had just marched 80 yards and were now 10 yards away from scoring what would be the winning touchdown, which would give us the opportunity to play in the state playoff game the following week. This was the most prestigious game you could play in junior college.

The next play would either be the final play of our season or for some of us, the last play of our careers. If we scored a touchdown, it would send us to the biggest game of our lives. I was being recruited by quite a few four-year colleges offering full football scholarships, and it was no secret that playing in and winning that state playoff game would definitely change the path my life would take. The last play of the game was a pass play. All of a sudden time slowed to a crawl. Even though thousands of spectators were roaring at the top of their lungs in anticipation of the outcome, I didn't hear them. My focus was on winning.

I dropped back to pass, looking for my wide receiver in the end zone. I couldn't see anyone that was open. I started to scramble out of the pocket (the area of protection the lineman provides for the quarterback). I wanted to buy more time in hopes that one of my receivers would somehow get open. But I still couldn't find any of my receivers. At that moment, I had to make a split decision. Instead of continuing to look for an open receiver, I decided I would take off running and try to score the winning touchdown myself.

Time has a strange way of playing tricks on your mind. As slowly as the final seconds of the game ticked by, in an instant it was all over. I came up short of scoring the game-winning touchdown by one yard. I couldn't believe it. I was so close yet so far away.

I was so disappointed, and what magnified my disappointment beyond words was that although I was certain there was no wide receiver open, and the choice I made to run for the winning touchdown was the right one, it wasn't. Turns out my favorite wide receiver, who had been a teammate of mine since my freshman year in high school, was wide open in the corner of the end zone.

How did I not see him? He was my "go-to guy" throughout my entire career. That game changed my life forever. I felt like it was my fault we lost. I couldn't help but think I let down my teammates, my coaches, the fans, and my family. The loss of that game tortured me both physically and emotionally and made me ache to my core for years. It ate me up like a flesh-eating disease. It's all I could think about. At this point in my life, and within three short years, I went from having some of the most exciting times to experiencing utter disappointment. Even though we didn't win that semifinal playoff game on that day, it didn't change the fact that we had a great season, with lots of wins and good memories. That said, what I find interesting was that as good as the wins always felt, the losses hurt much, much more. It's painful, but you have to address your failures in order to be successful. In other words, you must be willing to fail.

"Time heals," people say. My wounds in time did heal, but the scar remained. In the following months, just as I had hoped, universities came knocking. However, I was a bit disappointed that I didn't get more interest from some of the bigger powerhouse programs. It made me start thinking, what if we had won that semi playoff game and perhaps gone on to win state? Would I have gotten that full scholarship to the university I really wanted? If only I had seen my receiver in the corner of the end zone who was wide open.

My mind started getting the best of me. I had all of these negative thoughts buzzing around like a recorder running endlessly in my head. It got to the point where I thought somehow my future was jinxed because of the decision I made that had lost the game. I did realize in my limited objective thinking that I was being hard on myself and in fact that I alone really didn't lose the game. For example, one of my receivers who never bungled a pass the entire season dropped a touchdown pass earlier in the game.

In addition, we had more penalties called on us that day than we had all season, which could have potentially changed the outcome of the game. In fact had I seen the open receiver in the end zone, and if I had thrown to him, who knows that he wouldn't have dropped the pass? There were too many "ifs" to this scenario. But in my subjective state of mind, all I could think about was "what if?"

As it turned out, I was fortunate enough to get a full ride to Cal Poly Pomona University, which allowed me to keep alive my childhood dream of perhaps one day getting paid to play professionally. For the next couple of years, at least, I could continue to play the sport I loved so much.

CHAPTER SIX

The Day the Dream Died

Sometimes on the way to a dream you get lost and find a better one.

—Lisa Hammond, actress

Playing football at the university was not the same as playing in high school and junior college. In my hometown I was a big fish in a little pond, but now I was a little fish in a big pond, living 200 miles away from home for the first time. The thought of going away to school was exciting and shocking all at the same time. I'd never lived away from home or on my own. For the first time in my life, there would be no more parents telling me when to be home or asking where I'd been on a weekend.

A free man at last, or so I thought. After the newness of being on my own wore off, reality set in. Having new responsibilities made me realize what I had taken for granted all those years living at home. Washing my clothes, fending for my own food, waking up to my own alarm so I could make it to class on time, and doing homework all started cutting into my freedom.

In addition, even though I was fortunate to be on a full-ride scholarship playing the game I loved, I started to feel the pressure that came with it. Football was beginning to feel more like a job than a sport I simply enjoyed playing. When you're on scholarship you better perform and be on your best game week in and week out. There are several other players at your position who are just waiting to replace you. I did have moments where I really excelled. In fact, in my senior year in college, I was being mentioned throughout the league as a possible All-America candidate. As far as overall team success, however, it was disappointing. In the two years I was at Cal Poly, from 1975 to 1977, we never had a winning record. I had to deal with a lot more adversity than ever before in my sports career. My last two years of college were tumultuous, but one game changed the path of my life forever.

It was the last play of the first half, and the score was 14 to 3. We were down by 11 points. I was just about to throw a pass when the linebacker tackled me, driving me into the ground and crushing my chest. This knocked the wind out of me. I remember thinking I was going to die . . . right there. I'll never forget that moment. It was the first time I had ever been carried off the football field. After I regrouped, I stubbornly believed I could keep playing. I asked the trainer for some pain pills and went back out on the field to finish the second half. We redeemed ourselves and won the game 21 to 20. This was the greatest comeback of my football career, especially in the condition that I was in.

After the game was over, I didn't feel very well. My dad drove me home, and I started to feel worse. I felt a lot of pressure on my chest, like an elephant was sitting on me. A couple of hours went by and I continued to get worse, so my dad took me to the hospital. When we got there the doctor said he didn't think it was anything serious, maybe a broken rib. So I was sent back home and was forced to deal with the excruciating pain the entire weekend. I wasn't even able to lie down because of the intense pressure on my chest.

Monday finally came. I was driving myself to school and all of a sudden I felt extremely weak and started to pass out. Something was definitely wrong. I drove to the campus nurses' station, and they immediately sent me to the hospital. The doctors discovered I was bleeding internally. I had lost all but four pints of blood, had broken three ribs, and had a collapsed lung and broken artery. All the blood that I had lost was pushing my heart and lungs to the back of my body. The doctors rushed me into emergency surgery. They cut me open on the right side of my stomach, stuck a tube in, and started pumping the blood out of me. They did this for nine days. At the same time, they were giving me blood transfusions on the left side of my body.

This major injury was the straw that broke the camel's back. Even though it was serious and potentially life threatening, it wasn't career ending, and yet I decided that I wasn't going to play anymore. As I lay there in the hospital, getting blood transfusions and having a priest visit me on more than one occasion, I remember I wasn't afraid, nor did I think I was close to dying.

But as time passed and I recovered from my injury, I began to reflect. After the shock wore off, I became very afraid. My mind-set switched from being in the present to living in the past. I realized that I could have easily died. It had felt so strange to be in the moment like that and not be one bit afraid. The doctor told my dad that the only reason I didn't die was because I was an athlete and in good shape.

After this near-death experience I somehow convinced myself that this was a sign for me not to continue playing the sport I loved more than life itself. I had no idea that the choice I made would put me on a negative path, or so it seemed. But after a few years away from football, the thoughts that haunted my mind were that I really missed being an athlete and the excitement and adrenaline rush I got from playing in front of screaming fans. This was so seductive and incredibly addictive. Now it was all gone. I was like a junkie going through withdrawals.

Now I can admit that what I was doing back then was quitting. I quit on myself and I used the excuse of my injury to walk away from the sport. I told myself that the injury was a sign to get out. When the going gets tough, the tough get going, and I didn't allow myself to reach my full athletic potential. When things get hard we tend to withdraw because it takes more effort to fight for something than it does to just walk away.

I had no idea how much of an impact those three years would have on my life and the way I would respond to the great, good, rocky, and really bad times. For several years after college, I was lost. It was a wakeup call: after twelve years of playing sports, it was all over. As it turned out, making the decision to stop playing not only ended my football career; it also ended my childhood dream of one day becoming a professional athlete. I didn't realize how much that injury impacted me and never thought it would take me three months to start feeling good and like myself again.

When we're young, as I was at the time of this injury, we think we're invincible. This was my first real encounter with humble pie. As time went on I did in fact make a full physical recovery. The emotional impact, on the other hand, had a much greater effect on me. This was definitely a defining moment and marked a crossroad in my life, all at the age of 21.

My football picture sophomore year at College
of the Sequoias in my hometown Visalia.

CHAPTER SEVEN

Looking Back and Learning

Reflection is looking back so that the view looking forward is even clearer.

—Unknown

As I reflect back on Phase One of my life, I realize first and foremost I was fortunate and lucky enough to have sports early in my life, which became my foundation and provided stability. I learned important life lessons along the way. Each one helped me cope during a specific period of my personal life at a very critical time in my development. I could have gone down a dangerous path and gotten into a lot of trouble, which could have made me useless going into the later phases of my life.

Phase One revealed things about me that became very telling and created consistent personality traits I would be carrying for the rest of my life. I realized I had a tendency to be extreme, which was helpful but also had a destructive nature.

Perhaps the most important revelation was that when my back was against the wall and the chips were down, I could count on myself to come through. Phase One had its share of highs and lows, which is inevitable, and what impacted me most was my decision to stop chasing my childhood dream of becoming a pro athlete. The worst part was that I knew in my heart of hearts, I didn't try my best to reach my full athletic potential. I quit!

Doing things that are extraordinary requires passion. We must apply laser-beam focus to an objective, no matter how long it takes, and yet there are never any guarantees that we will succeed. At times this is a harsh reality and stops people from reaching their potential. Failure is a big part of success. History proves that some of life's biggest success stories happened as a result of failure, and most of the time, because of many failures. Success can be learned with the help of life lessons, and we must be willing to endure.

Phase Two

Twenty-One to Twenty-Eight Years Old

CHAPTER EIGHT

Life After Sports

New beginnings are often disguised as painful endings.

—Lao Tzu

I decided that my next move was to get out in the real world and get a job. But it occurred to me that due to the fact that from the ages of eight through 20, except for little odd jobs my coaches got me at school, the only job I ever had was working on our family dairy farm.

I was born and raised on a dairy farm and had plenty of work experience, better defined as cheap labor. I had to do chores before and after school, as well as on the weekends. This was common practice in that world, especially with family-owned dairies. In hindsight it wasn't a bad thing, because it taught me not to be afraid of work. However at this point in my life, I wasn't ready to go back to the dairy lifestyle.

Being away from football gave me a whole new perspective on my life. Even though there was a family dairy farm I could fall back on, it was not my first choice. At least not yet. My first real job after sports, then, was masonry construction. I got the job through one of my teammates.

My job description was to be a "gofer." It means go for this, go for that. In other words, tough manual labor. I was at the beck and call of the person who ran the masonry crew, which consisted of five of us. We all were around the same age and all were ex-athletes. Even though it was hard manual work for a first job, I liked it. It was something brand new, so I had a lot to learn, plus I was working alongside guys who were competitive, which made work fun.

My boss was a Canadian ex-hockey player whose name was Reggie. He was a good boss who was tough and expected a lot from us, but most of all he was fair. At this time in my life, this job was just what I needed. It was a good outlet and distraction that kept my mind off of dealing with the fact that my sports career was really over.

Years after football was over I could not bear even to watch the game I loved so much. Not only could I not bring myself to attend a local high school or college football game, I couldn't even watch a game on TV. I really began to think I had made a big mistake walking away from the sport when I did. I kept thinking and asking myself, what if? What if I had continued to pursue my lifelong childhood dream to become a pro athlete? What would have happened? How would that have changed my life? The real truth is that based on statistics, it was a long shot at best to make it to that elite level.

But that made less of a difference to me than thinking that maybe, just maybe I would have been one of the chosen few who beat the odds. As the years rolled by these voices in my head only got louder. This led me down a path of doubt and frustration. Now that I have hindsight to help me evaluate that period, it has become very obvious I sold myself short, at least in the pursuit of reaching my full athletic potential.

For seven years, my decision to quit football haunted me. The only way I finally moved on was to make myself a promise that if somehow, some way I ever got another opportunity to have the kind of feeling the sport of football gave me, I would willingly pursue it with a vengeance. I would not quit or walk away until I did whatever it took to reach my full potential. This pact I made with myself helped calm the restless bear inside me, at least for the time being.

It was time for me to deal with the next segment of my life. It was important for me to become proactive and move forward, no matter how painful it all felt. The longer I was around masonry, the more I wanted to learn. After about a year I decided I wanted to be in charge of my own crew, which meant becoming a mason. It would be like being the quarterback of my team. I liked working alongside my crew members as a mason's helper; however, I really wanted to be the mason at some point because of the opportunity to make more money and be the leader of my own crew, or team. I was learning and doing something new. My juices were flowing.

Becoming a mason taught me something I didn't know about myself. I had a creative side, and I was able to express my creativity through my work. To be able to construct something from scratch and turn it into something beautiful was extremely satisfying. Then to see the satisfaction on the customer's face was icing on the cake and a big boost to my ego. The next several years in masonry were a bit of a growing period.

Learning about a new industry other than the dairy business and sports widened my horizons. I began to realize that even though my sports career was over, and even though I still had complicated feelings about how it ended, I used the lessons I learned from sports to help me excel as a mason. I realized that sports would be the foundation on which I would build the rest of my life.

In the spirit of adventure and self-exploration, I decided to spread my wings a little more. Football was a very physical sport, and I loved the contact, but there was a part of me that wondered if I was ever in a situation where I had to fight and defend myself when there was no other alternative, how would I respond? Up to this point in my life, I had never been in a fight. I truly believe that part of the reason was that I never went looking for one. I also think that being an athlete builds confidence and self-esteem. I think people can sense that and perceive you as someone who shouldn't be messed with.

I certainly was happy about that, but I still wondered about my capabilities, so I decided to find out. I moved to Newport Beach and got a job as a bouncer. I brilliantly deduced that as a bouncer, at some point, I would end up in a fight. Added benefits included lots of beautiful women, and I would be living at the beach. At least this was my perception of my new job. I was now working by day as a mason in Los Angeles and by night as a bouncer in Newport Beach. My work schedule suddenly became very hectic, but I wasn't going to give up my mason job because it was definitely more lucrative.

I worked my mason job Monday through Saturday, 6 am to 4 pm, and my bouncing job schedule was Tuesday through Saturday, 8:30 pm to 2 am. Needless to say, I became sleep deprived and life got even more challenging. As I suspected, I did end up getting into a fight as a bouncer, and it happened within the first two weeks. I had to kick a guy out of the bar for harassing a waitress. I was scared out of my mind before it all went down. But fear is a positive motivator. I told him I needed to talk to him outside, where it was quieter. Getting him outside was a way to level the playing field. Still, I trembled. When I told him that he wasn't going back in, the game was on. He flinched, and my survival instincts helped me take him out. I was shaking uncontrollably, but I found out how I would respond when push came to shove. By nature, I'm not confrontational; however, what I learned about myself was how strong my survival instincts were.

I worked as a bouncer for almost two years and had lots of confrontations. I never got my butt kicked, but there were some scary close calls. As I had hoped, the benefits of being around beautiful women more than made up for this. When you're a bouncer, girls want to know and be with you because of benefits like getting in the club without waiting in line. It was a great perk, but it took its toll on me because of all the afterparties. It got to the point where having two jobs and too many beautiful girls meant I was sleeping only every other night.

Me in my heyday after college.

Within six months of burning the candle at both ends, I had lost a lot of weight and had very dark circles under my eyes. I didn't realize how bad I looked until I went back home to visit, and my dad asked, "What the hell's wrong with you, you got cancer?"

To paraphrase another saying, sometimes you can't see the forest for the trees. Throw in a good dose of denial to cloud judgment even further. I thought I was fine. But all good things must come to an end. DARN! It wasn't long after my dad's perceptive observation that I made a decision to change the path I was on. I reluctantly quit the bouncing job and decided to move away from the beach, where so many beautiful girls were, to be closer to my day job as a mason. Even though bouncing had its perks, it didn't have the long-term potential that masonry offered.

This being said, I still wasn't ready to give up bouncing altogether. I found another bouncing job closer to my day job. That lasted another year before I gave up bouncing for good. I started having nightmares about angry patrons whom I had tossed out of the nightclub, or had gotten in a fight with, coming back after hours to get revenge.

This actually happened to me quite a few times. More than once I had to stay inside the nightclub and have the police called because of someone who came back with a gun. People do some pretty stupid things, especially when alcohol is involved. The main reasons I chose to bounce were to live by the beach, test my survival skills, and meet beautiful women. Mission accomplished, and then some.

Bouncing taught me how to deal with people effectively, even when they were on their worst behavior. A good example of this occurred when I was first learning to be a bouncer. I was constantly getting into altercations with both men and women. As time passed and I gained more on-the-job experience, the fights and altercations dramatically decreased.

Interestingly enough, the only difference between my early days when I was constantly fighting and later when those altercations dramatically decreased, was what I learned to do. I still had to deal with the same types of people in the same environment; however, I learned to adapt in moments of confrontation and could usually prevent potential problems. I became a master at verbal and nonverbal communication and learned to manipulate people and situations effectively by the selection of words used and messages communicated with my body language. In addition, I was able to decipher the verbal and nonverbal messages people were communicating to me.

It's amazing how powerful this process is. I found it fascinating and learned that approximately sixty percent of how people communicate is nonverbally. Learning this amazing technique of determining what people are really saying has benefited me throughout my entire life. Life keeps teaching us lessons and providing tools to prepare us for what's up ahead. At times it really does seem like there is a method to the madness.

Shortly before my bouncing stint came to an end, I met a girl. Wen was a waitress at a restaurant where I hung out. We got to know each other and soon discovered that we shared a birthday although she was a year younger. That's when we felt there was some kind of unspoken connection. Unlike so many of the other girls I met and had a good time with during my crazy days as a bouncer, there was something different about Wen. A lot of the girls that came into the nightclub wanted to be picked up, but she wasn't that type of person. She also had an easiness about her. I felt comfortable with her. I hadn't felt that with anyone else before.

Turns out the spark I felt became a flame, and within a couple of years we were married. Now that I was in a serious relationship, I started thinking more about my future. I really enjoyed being a mason and seriously considered making a career out of it, but my instincts told me otherwise.

I felt frustrated and uncertain, and I didn't like that. I was bothered by the fact that if I made my career as a mason, I would have a better chance of living in the Los Angeles area. I might have been looking too far ahead, but raising kids in L.A. was not something I wanted to do. As it turns out, I stayed in the masonry business and in the Los Angeles area for five more years. My life at this point was in transition. After going back and forth about which path I should travel, I decided to move back to my hometown with my new wife to work on the family dairy farm. But I was torn.

CHAPTER NINE

Taking the Bull by the Horns

If you get a second chance, take it.

—Leo Costa, Jr.

A part of me knew coming back to my hometown and working on the family dairy farm was the right thing in terms of raising a family. I definitely knew I didn't want to raise kids in a big city. The other part of me felt like I settled, because in my heart of hearts I knew the dairy business wasn't in my blood. It would be a job that gave me a steady paycheck. I tried to love it, but I just couldn't. After a few years I became increasingly unhappy, and once again I became frustrated and angry.

The bear inside of me started roaring and the buried, unresolved feelings of quitting on my dream to be a pro athlete started bubbling back up to the surface. Except this time, the haunting noises in my head were much louder. By the time I was 38 years old, I'd had enough of trying to make the dairy business my way of life. I now had two young boys and had been married for six years. I had gotten into working out with weights a couple of years prior, primarily because I was in the worst shape of my life. This was a first for me considering that as an athlete for thirteen years, I was always in pretty top shape.

I never had done any serious weight training before, but I really started liking how lifting weights was making me feel and, eventually, making me look. Life has some interesting twists, turns, and surprises. As I continued to get in better shape, I continued to get more excited about weight training. I started getting some fire in my belly, something I hadn't felt since I had played football. Before I knew it I was reading muscle magazines to see what I could learn and what was needed to get in better shape. I felt an obsession coming on. My weight-training objective evolved from lifting to tightening, toning, and conditioning my body and eventually to packing on muscle.

I was very fascinated by the articles I was reading in the muscle magazines and astonished by the cartoon-like bodies some of the bodybuilders had created. I wasn't really sure if I liked that look, but I assumed it must have taken an enormous amount of hard work and effort to get like that. I had no idea!

After about a year of training in my garage, it was time to join a gym or a health club where there was more equipment, which I needed to continue to get the kind of results I wanted. As I learned more and more about training to pack on muscle, I realized that there was way more to learn. In a nutshell, I needed to add two more components to my weight-training regimen: nutrition and cardiovascular conditioning. Little did I know the can of worms I was opening for myself. I was slowly getting into the sport of bodybuilding, and I didn't even know it. What I did know was I liked working out with weights and the way it was making me look and feel.

I was also attracted to the fact that it was difficult. It wasn't easy getting my body to change, especially to add muscle. As I began to learn more about weight training, cardiovascular conditioning, and nutrition, it was obvious that all three components would play an important role in the results I might want. Learning about bodybuilding and making progress on my development, I noticed I started getting more and more attention from people in the gym where I was training. They asked me lots of questions about what I was doing to get the rapid results I was attaining.

The more people inquired about my training, the more it spurred me on. I was hungry to learn everything I could, not only for myself, but also for the people who were interested enough to come ask for my advice and opinion. I was flattered and shocked at the same time. I was also hungry for more. There was a fire starting to burn in my gut, which got my blood boiling. I felt like I was coming alive again.

Russ Horine was the instructor at Sequoia Athletic Club, the health club where I was training, who was responsible for assisting people if they needed to be watched while performing an exercise. He had noticed how hard I pushed myself in my training and at some point had introduced himself.

We hit it off right away. He seemed to know a lot about training and nutrition, which was what I needed. A few months of training at my new health club, learning more and more from Russ, fueled the fire in my belly. I started falling in love with bodybuilding. Eventually, Russ became my friend, training partner, and my current business partner. Within a year of consistent, serious training and with a lot of encouragement from Russ, I entered my first bodybuilding competition. In a million years I never thought I would ever get up on a stage in front of screaming fans in a bikini, posing to music no less, while having judges critique me.

A part of me was excited about competing, but the other part of me was freaked out. When I was in school I avoided any classes that required oral presentations, and now I was going to compete in a bikini for all to see. That first bodybuilding competition did in fact freak me out, but I loved it. I had abstained from any temptations and overcome months of suffering to get up on stage. I had also overcome one of my biggest fears: being on stage in front of people. I did surprisingly well. I couldn't wait to get back to the gym to start improving on the areas that were lagging. I knew I wanted to compete again. There was no doubt in my mind that I was hooked on bodybuilding.

My first bodybuilding competition in 1982. I was competing at the Mr. Visalia show (novice division) at the age of 27.

That competition changed my life forever. So many years had passed since I had played football and built up all the frustration of how it ended. Still, the bittersweet feelings kept resurfacing, which at times felt as if there was a bear inside of me, roaring. It was very unsettling and it caused me to act out in different ways. I hated when the bear would return, and it often did. I knew down deep I hadn't been happy since I gave up my childhood dream of being a pro athlete, and it became more apparent the more I immersed myself in bodybuilding. After three years of training and three competitions, I knew in my gut this was my second chance. I was again pursuing a passion.

I was 28 years old and newly married with two very young children. I had a decision to make. Did I stay at the family dairy business where I was getting a steady paycheck, or did I pursue starting my own business as a personal trainer?

Family picture with my two sons, Shane (right) and Josh (left).

I was taking a big chance considering that having a personal trainer was really only popular in the bigger cities like Los Angeles or San Francisco. I lived in neither place. To add even more pressure, the family business was generally passed down from generation to generation. Taking it over was, to an extent, expected of me. No matter which decision I made, someone was going to get hurt. In the end it really came down to whether I wanted to stay in a family business that offered a good livelihood but was more of a job for which I had very little or no passion, or to follow my gut and the promise I made to myself years earlier. I had decided that if I ever got a second opportunity to do something that gave me the passion football did, I would seize the moment.

I seized the moment! I was going into uncharted waters in terms of knowing how to start and grow a business. I would have to figure all this out on my own and on the fly, with a lot of trial and error. Nothing in this life is one hundred percent guaranteed but taxes and death. I knew there was a chance my venture would fail, but the thought of how painful my life would be if I didn't give my new business a try didn't even compare to being in a job that was just a job. Once again I was at another crossroads, and I was entering into Phase Three of my life.

Phase Two had been a total transitional period. I was a newlywed with young children, trying to figure out if the family business was really what I wanted to do for the rest of my life. All I was doing was working, and consequently letting myself go. The one shining light during this period was that I discovered the sport of bodybuilding. I also learned something about human nature that directly applied to me. I discovered that we become more proactive when both pain and pleasure are present in our lives.

Phase Three

Twenty-Eight Years Old to Present

CHAPTER TEN

Perfect Willingness

If you want something you've never had, you must be willing to do something you've never done.

—Thomas Jefferson

All of my life lessons would come into play for me to take on the most exciting and challenging times I could have ever imagined. When I first went out on my own, I had to supplement personal training by working for my in-laws in their restaurant as a short-order cook. It wasn't something I wanted to do, but I would do what I had to until my personal training business took off. You have to have perfect willingness and be willing to sacrifice to get what you want. The X factor for me was the passion I had for my bodybuilding and new personal training business.

Being self-employed has its upsides, no doubt, but there are no nets in which to fall. Working as an employee, you have the security of a steady paycheck. There were a lot of challenging and scary times during the building of my business, wondering whether I was going to make it. Having a family was powerful motivation and a reminder that I had to make it, and I somehow managed to pull through. Thanks to my determination and perseverance, my personal training business did in fact take off. I had to constantly adapt and change my strategy to keep pushing forward. I was then ready to take my personal training business and bodybuilding career to the next level, so I did.

The next level of my evolution as a bodybuilder was to take my body to a new state of conditioning. As an athlete, I was used to being challenged, and I loved competing. The fact that one has to have persistence and the motivation to perfect one's craft is what always attracted me to any sport I played. I liked the challenge. That's why I was attracted to the sport of bodybuilding. It takes years to get your body in the kind of condition required to compete. It's not unusual for someone to take 12 to 15 years to achieve the quality to compete at the world level, which is where I was determined to be.

Competing at a higher level would eventually force me to make a difficult decision if I wanted to be a contender. I would have to take performance-enhancing drugs. In my early years of bodybuilding I was determined to compete naturally. My initial strategy was to learn everything I could about how the body worked and the kind of training methodologies that would be most efficient so I could get maximum results.

The first three years of my training were very productive, and I was having reasonable success competing in bodybuilding competitions at the local level. The fourth year was a crossroads because I wanted to compete at the regional level, and I knew competition would be much stiffer. I had to find competitions that were considered natural, which meant the athletes would be drug tested. I competed in my first regional competition as a natural athlete and came in looking good. At this time, though, I noticed that some of the bodybuilders I competed against not only looked better, but the quality of their physiques also had a different look. They had more muscle mass and looked more conditioned. I went on to discover that even though the competition was supposed to be drug free, it wasn't. That explained why some of the competitors had a different look to them.

The reality was that the competitors had a way to beat the drug test. So now my real options were to compete on an uneven playing field, to stop competing, or to take performance-enhancing drugs. If I wanted to compete at the higher level, I would have to take the drugs. So I asked myself a question. What was my specific goal? It was to compete and win at the world level where I could turn pro, which would be a childhood dream come true. I then had to make a tough decision. Before I decided to start enhancing, I did my research and educated myself on the risks versus the rewards. Some risks included potential liver damage and torn muscle. When you tear a muscle, you actually pull the tendon off the bone and it can rupture, which is a significant injury. This requires surgery to take that muscle and put it back on the bone. That was my biggest concern. Except for those two risks, I didn't give a shit. I gave up on my dream once, and I refused to do it again. I was so close to reaching my goal, and I had perfect willingness to do whatever it took to succeed. Nothing was going to stop me, not even myself.

After adding a performance-enhancing program, the difference from one year to the next was significant. It accelerated muscle growth and dramatically improved recovery, which gave me a competitive edge. I know this will go against popular belief, but there is a misconception that because you're taking performance-enhancing drugs you require less effort to get the same results. That's incorrect and misleading. You still have to do the work. I competed at the national level and took first place in the heavyweight division. After I won at the national level, I become much more popular. I was featured in the local newspaper and received attention from national media through bodybuilding muscle magazines. But when I started gaining more attention, I became a bigger target for people to take down. This can be contradictory in a way because when I got to this level, I was exposed to the public in some ways that could be more harmful to my health than the drug use.

Me at a photo shoot in my old gym, Optimum
Training Techniques in Visalia, California.

To take my business to the next level, I felt I needed to become more unique. I decided the way to do this was by learning more about cutting-edge training methodologies. This led me to create a unique style of personal training after a tour I took to Bulgaria and Russia. It was the first symposium where Americans were allowed to watch the Bulgarian Olympic weightlifting team perform up close and in person. It was kept very hush hush, and it promised to be a one-time opportunity to talk to the Olympic coaches and sport doctors to learn the secrets of their success. I saw this advertisement in a muscle magazine, and without hesitation, I sent in my resume. About a month later, I was selected. This tour changed my life forever. I had no idea what the next nine years would hold for my business and bodybuilding career. I was on a fast track to living the dream, and then some luck came my way.

One night when I was watching a movie called *The Untouchables* I noticed one of the actors on the screen looked familiar, but I couldn't place him. After the movie was over, I ran into a schoolmate of mine and asked him if he knew who he was. He looked at me and laughed, "That's Kevin Costner. We went to school with him." Then it hit me! He went to my high school for one year, and we played baseball together. I knew exactly who he was. We were good friends back in our younger days. I ended up calling his studio in Hollywood and left a message with the front desk to tell him Leo Costa called. Four days later, I received a phone call from Kevin himself. I asked him how he was doing and told him that I had just seen him on the big screen. When the hell did that happen? We caught up and he told me about his new career. I told him I was in the personal training business, competing in bodybuilding competitions and writing training manuals. At the time, I had just finished my first bodybuilding training manual called *Bulgarian Burst*, which was going to be sold worldwide. I asked him if he would be willing to let me use his name as a testimonial. He was all for it, and it just so happened at this time that he was producing and acting in a movie called *Dances with Wolves*. He asked me to come down and train him for the movie. That was the beginning of the next level for me.

Kevin Costner (an old high school buddy) and I hanging
out at an after party following one of his concerts at the
Tachi Palace Hotel and Casino in Lemoore, California.

Through Kevin I met many different famous people, started training professional athletes, and began attending premieres and going to
afterparties. He was also generous enough to get me an opportunity to
audition for a part in the movie *The Bodyguard*, for a character named
Frank. I went in and realized at that point I wasn't cut out to be an
actor. They make it look so easy, but it's definitely harder than it looks.
I was in a small room by myself when two people entered. The woman
asked me if I had studied my lines, and I said yes. She then asked me
if I was ready to go, and again I said yes. The minute she said action,
I choked. Not only did I choke then, but I choked a second time.
Afterward, I called Kevin and thanked him for the opportunity. I knew
at that point I needed to stick with what I did best, bodybuilding and
personal training, but I did start to get a taste for the celebrity life.

A year later my bodybuilding started taking off. I was on a tour in
Germany at Health Fibo where I was lucky enough to meet a gentleman
named Tom Platz. In those days, Tom was the second most noted professional bodybuilder in the world. Tom and Arnold Schwarzenegger
competed against one another for many years. I went on this tour in
hopes of connecting with a big name in the sport of bodybuilding,
somebody who could endorse and help further promote my manuals.

I seized the moment! I had to do some quick work, because I was there for only a couple of weeks. I took Tom aside and gave him some background information. I mentioned that I was an up-and-coming author, bodybuilder, and personal trainer who had just written another training manual called *Big Beyond Belief.* He was very interested in my work, but Tom was still under contract for another year with the World Bodybuilding Federation. He was unable to come aboard at that time. But it all happened a year later. That was the best decision I could have made for my bodybuilding career. During that time Tom took me under his wing and taught me everything he knew about bodybuilding, promoting, and being in the big time.

We hired a promoter who brought us to Europe to do a tour and market *Big Beyond Belief.* We were traveling all over Europe, stopping in France, Germany, and Belgium. We were doing store openings, seminars, and posing exhibitions. This time in our lives changed us both. We learned a lot from each other. When we were in France, we were treated like rock stars. People would flock to us because of Tom. For example, when we ate lunch we had to be protected by bodyguards to keep fans from grabbing at us. I remember it like it was yesterday. We were sitting in the middle of a security circle and hands would be reaching out for us. I thought it was awesome but kind of scary. It's weird to have people looking at you while you're eating, but after a while, you get used to it. It was awesome but eerie. Tom was so used to it, but to me it was very new. Through him, I was associated with that rock-star lifestyle. It was crazy.

Photo shoot at Gold's Gym in Venice Beach, California with
Tom Platz, promoting my training manual Big Beyond Belief.

At one of the posing exhibitions, we had 5,000 enthusiastic fans
come to see us perform. Five thousand! Tom and I would go on stage
and perform a choreographed skit. We would pose together with music
and show people our bodies, much like what we would do at a bodybuilding competition. They would scream and cheer us on while admir-
ing our physiques. It was intoxicating. This was such an amazing experience. We did this for about a year. I eventually became a well-known
author of best-selling bodybuilding training manuals. After our tour
in Europe, Tom and I continued training together. I traveled to Venice
Beach, California, for three months and stayed at the Marina Pacific
Hotel. This hotel was very close to where Tom lived, as well as to Gold's
Gym, known as the mecca of bodybuilding. This was where most of
the pro bodybuilders or anyone who wanted to be around them came
to train, including movie stars, producers, and Hollywood executives.
It was a freak show, and I was in it. I loved it. With his knowledge and
guidance, Tom took my body to the next level. He taught me things

about training that would have taken years to learn, putting me on a fast track to the national and world levels of bodybuilding. He was a huge influence on me.

During this time Tom had gotten into some part-time acting and had an opportunity to play a starring role in a movie that was being produced for the Cannes Film Festival, an international cultural event in France. He asked me if I wanted to play a small part in the movie and the first thing I thought about was my failed acting debut with Kevin Costner. However, the part I was playing with Tom was a non-speaking role. I figured I couldn't screw that up, so I went for it. I was a doorman. My job was to stand outside the door of a house holding a gun. I helped break down the door and dragged a guy out who had just gotten shot. That was the end of my acting career.

I continued traveling the globe, giving seminars, doing posing exhibitions, and touching so many people's lives with training information they wanted specifically from me. It was such a flattering and humbling experience. I made a promise to myself years before that if something came along that gave me the fire in the belly like football did, I would not make the same mistake as I had in my twenties and sell myself short. So I didn't.

Tom Platz, Don Ross and I after enjoying a meal at The Firehouse Restaurant in Venice Beach, California. This was a restaurant where all the famous bodybuilders went to eat.

Photoshoot at Gold's Gym in Venice Beach, California with
Tom Platz prior to my upcoming bodybuilding competition.

This was me right before competing at the
Mr. World Competition in Belgium, Europe.

Shooting for the top — Leo Costa Jr. of Visalia is aiming to capture a spot in the Mr. Universe show, the world's highest-ranking event for amateur bodybuilders. The 5-foot-10 Costa weighs 260 pounds, with just seven percent body fat.

Roger Jerkovich/Times-Delta

Hobby becomes huge for bodybuilder

By Scott Sellman
Times-Delta

The rigors of training have definitely paid off for one Leo Costa Jr.

Costa, who's been banging the weights for 14 years, will be competing in the National Amateur Bodybuilding Association USA Nationals on Sept. 3 in Alameda.

With 12 states being represented, placing in the top two or three will probably qualify him for the Mr. Universe show Oct. 8 in England. That is the world's highest-ranking amateur event.

Costa qualified for the Nationals with a second-place finish at the Mr. Western USA show last year.

The 5-foot-10 Costa weighs in at 260 pounds, with just seven percent body fat. He'll trim down to 247-250 for the Nationals contest with about five percent body fat.

■ More on Costa: Personal gym becomes thriving business/4B

"I'm in much better shape than I was last year [when he qualified]," said Costa. "Last year I weighed in at 235."

These upcoming contests could vault Costa into the pro level of bodybuilding.

"From a competitive standpoint," said Costa, "I've always wanted to be a professional athlete. This is an avenue to reach that goal."

The quarterback for Cal Poly Pomona in 1977-78, Costa did not start weightlifting until the age of 25.

"[Coaches] then didn't have the information [that they now have] in my day," said Costa, 39.

"As a quarterback, I was al-

lergic to weights because my coaches made us stay away from them. The weights were only for the lineman."

So how did he start?

"I was just trying to get in shape before I got married," he said. "I wanted to look good in my tuxedo."

The casual interest got serious in a hurry.

"Once I started, I got hooked," he said.

"Then the competitive juices started flowing. There's just a certain high you get when you compete."

His first contest in 1982, the Mr. Visalia, he took second at age 28.

He later placed third in the Mr. Central California show.

"I didn't compete much [after that] because I was too busy with my [personal train-

ing] business. Now that the business is doing so well, I can now focus on the competitive side."

"I'm not doing this for the money," he adds. "This is something I love and it's a way to reach my personal goal of getting to the pro status. In the meantime, it gives credibility to the books and videos that I do."

In addition to authoring books, putting together videos and conducting a large mail-order business, Costa has personal columns in both Muscular Development and Ironman magazines. He will soon have another in Muscle Mag.

Costa's pre-contest regimen includes working out 2-3 times a day — six days a week, and doing half an hour of aerobics every day.

Local newspaper article promoting my personal training business Optimum Training Techniques located in Visalia, California.

At this time I was in the moment and giving it everything I had. It was intoxicating living the life I had always dreamed about. I loved it and couldn't possibly get enough. When you get the kind of attention and adulation I was receiving, it can at times blindside you because you lose perspective. But life has its way of keeping you grounded.

Earlier in this story I mentioned the four important life lessons I learned through the different phases of my life, and how they would all become present in Phase Three. As much as it took believing in myself, having a good work ethic, and being humbled or getting humbled in order to achieve what I was able to do at this point in Phase Three, the life lesson that got my undivided attention was number four, perfect willingness.

I was now 41 years of age and decided to retire from the sport of bodybuilding. I had a good run, but it was time. Being on the road and gone as much as I was took a toll on my personal life. I ended up going through a divorce. It should have stayed between Wen and myself, but instead it became very public. Divorce is never easy and I know that from firsthand experience, but this went way beyond where it should have gone. I was arrested in broad daylight.

Before all of this went down, I had gotten word from a close friend that I should watch my back because the local police were keeping an eye on me. I never had any run-in or issues with the police in all my years in business. At this point, my personal training business had been at the same location for about 15 years.

As soon as I got wind of this information, I personally called the police department and asked if they had something they wanted to talk to me about. I offered to come down and answer any questions. I wanted to be proactive because initially in our divorce Smitty, my ex-father-in-law, threatened me on more than one occasion. He even came into my place of business to let me know, and I quote, "I'm going to take you out if it's the last thing I do."

I made it a point never to respond to his threats, because I really did understand that he was angry at me for hurting his daughter. I was a bit concerned though, because my former father-in-law was very good friends with the police sergeant who ate in his restaurant on a regular basis. There was, to a degree, a "good old boy" attitude in my hometown. I was suspicious, maybe even a bit paranoid, that strings would be pulled to make my life miserable. Otherwise, why all of a sudden was I being warned that the police were watching me? I may have been trying to connect dots that weren't there.

Nevertheless, the result of my proactive phone call with the police department ended with them stating there was no need for me to come down to answer any questions. However and not coincidentally, it wasn't long after the phone call that the police, in what seemed like a staged event and a sting operation, arrested me in broad daylight on a busy street, and simultaneously raided my personal training studio during business hours.

I was that evening's top television news story and the following morning's front-page news in the local newspaper. I guess the dots I was trying to connect, which seemed far away, were closer than I thought. My suspicion that I was set up was confirmed by more than one policeman who worked for the department during that time when they arrested me. Guess I was right about the good old boy system. This nightmare all happened because of a divorce that went horribly wrong. I was the bad guy in the split because I'm the one that wanted out. I had to get out. I knew I couldn't be faithful or happy as I had already strayed more than once in our 18-year marriage. It was not fair to Wen, or our kids, to hurt them anymore. Obviously, I had my own unresolved issues I needed to sort out.

I left the marriage with only my clothes and my car and started a new life. This is when it all got crazy and personal. Over the next six months my condo and gym were broken into, and I received threats from my ex-father-in-law to the point that I had to get a restraining order. My ex-father-in-law and ex-wife were on a mission to destroy me. I honestly don't think my ex really wanted to see me burn on the cross as her dad did, but she did get caught up in the chaos her dad was causing. Smitty was a very controlling person in general but even more so with his family, especially his children. They feared him and lived with a tremendous amount of guilt.

One day Smitty had gotten wind from Wen that his son Larz was taking steroids. When Smitty confronted and threatened Larz and pressured him to tell him where he got the steroids, my ex-brother-in-law lied and said he had gotten them from me. Several months later, Larz went as far as lying under oath when he was called to testify against me in court. He saved his own ass and threw me under the bus. I wasn't surprised Wen followed along and Larz caved when his dad pressured him. They were out to ruin me, and I vowed that it would be a cold day in hell before I would cave. When it was all said and done I would prevail, and in the end I did.

I went to hell and back for two years, but they didn't take me out or ruin me. Far from it. The next two years of my life turned out to be the biggest nightmare ever. I was fighting battles in court on two fronts simultaneously. In criminal court, I was charged with several felony counts of drug charges, which included selling, transporting, distributing, and possessing steroids. If convicted I could spend up to 20 years in prison. On the second front, in divorce court, I was defending and fighting for my life against one of the most noted divorce attorneys known for going straight for the jugular vein.

In addition, I had taken a major hit professionally. After my very public arrest, the first question I had to answer was should I close my personal training studio or go on with business as usual. I reasoned that if I closed my business, it would give the perception that I was guilty and that they had won. I wasn't guilty, no matter how incorrectly the press portrayed me.

I decided to go on with business as usual. The first day I walked into my personal training studio after my arrest was one of the most awkward experiences in my life. I was barraged with a lot of questions and concerns from my clients. My strategy was to address all questions and be honest. What I learned was that with the exception of only a few people, my clients supported me. They were definitely concerned that I would be able to survive and remain open. However, my clients expressed that they believed in me, not the rumors. They felt what I was being accused of was not true.

This support was huge, which made me feel like I had a fighting chance. My personal training business now became my safe haven, a fortress where I could circle the wagons and prepare for war. My immediate challenge would be to get things back to normal and gain people's trust again, not so much the clients who stayed with me but rather the potential clients who were now staying away. Some people were skeptical, others were judging me, and I could tell when I was out in public that some even hated me.

One thing I learned was that when you go through a bad divorce, let alone a criminal drug investigation, you polarize people. You find out in a hurry who your real friends are, as well as the ones who are fickle. Some of the friends that I shared with my ex-wife felt like because of the divorce, they had to choose whom they would remain friends with. Some people who read and saw all of the press about the steroid investigation were certain I was guilty without really knowing the truth. During this tumultuous time, I learned a lot about people and my capability to endure.

Three months passed after my arrest before any new clients started coming to my business. It was painstaking, but in time I got my business on a somewhat stable terrain. I still was in the middle of two public court battles. I didn't know if I was going to be found innocent or guilty of the steroid allegations, and I was trying to survive the Rambo-like tactics my ex-wife and her attorney were unleashing. My future loomed ahead, filled with uncertainty. The thought of spending time in prison or losing everything I had and being forced out on the street was horrifying. I lost a lot of sleep and aged tremendously over this.

On a personal level, I took a stand and knew if I didn't believe in myself no one else would. From the first day when I was portrayed in the media to be a big drug kingpin, I made sure that I never hid or withdrew from being out in public and doing the normal things like going to my kids' games or going to a movie. One of the hardest things I've ever had to do was face people who didn't know how to act or what to say to me. It was also very awkward in public when I could see and hear people talking about me, even staring at me like I was some sort of a monster.

My strategy and ongoing philosophy in life thereafter would be to stay true to myself and carry on, not letting my circumstances change me unless it was a positive change. The more I forced myself to live my life and carry on in public, the more I could feel the perception of what people thought and how they felt about me. In fact, it got to the point that my life was like a *Rocky* movie where overcoming all odds would be the ultimate test. Strangely, it felt like some people we're getting behind me in their support. They made comments like "Hang in there" or "I'm praying for you." Life is one giant classroom with lessons to be taught and learned. Sometimes truth is stranger than fiction, and I lived it firsthand.

When the cops raided my personal training studio, it became front-page headline news. The police told the reporter that they thought they had found steroids, when in fact what they found were herbs from Bulgaria. They also mentioned they believed they found a list of people I sold these steroids to, when in fact what they were referring to were the waivers clients signed before they joined, which basically stated they were healthy enough to exercise. Finally, they found a book that I had written called *The Anabolic Diet*. I sold this book worldwide for years. In it I wrote about a specific way to eat FOOD for bodybuilding performance, but the police said that this book was the way I taught people how to use steroids. As part of the front-page news, which featured a big color photo of me and the story, the reader also saw a picture of the waivers, the herbs, and *The Anabolic Diet*. How the police and newspaper tried to portray me in that article was inaccurate, but they were able to get away with it because of certain words they used such as "they believe," and "allegedly."

LOCAL/3A

Mothers in jail get special visit

SPORTS/1B

49ers beat Broncos, gain homefield edge

LIFESTYLE/6B

Seasonal stress can be avoided

VISALIA TIMES-DELTA

DECEMBER 16, 1997 TUESDAY A GANNETT NEWSPAPER • 50 CENTS

Chamber names its new executive director

New leader — Ken Oplinger sits at the head of the Visalia Chamber of Commerce's boardroom table.

Fremont's director of governmental affairs will take over Jan. 5

By Brett Tam
Times-Delta

The Visalia Chamber of Commerce has chosen a new executive director.

Ken Oplinger will become the chamber's president/chief executive officer Jan. 5. He works for the Fremont Chamber of Commerce, where he is the director of governmental affairs.

Oplinger, a Tempe, Ariz., native, was selected from more than 30 applications by an eight-member search committee. He accepted the job Friday, said Sharon Stenger, chamber interim executive director.

"Ken's a professional. He's a quick study, articulate and a good communicator," said Amy Pack, chairwoman of the search committee and Times-Delta publisher. "His knowledge and experience, along with his wit and enthusiasm, will take the Visalia Chamber of Commerce to a new level."

Others on the search committee: Visalia City Manager Steve Salomon; Charley Clouse, principal of the Transportation Planning Group, Mike Chrisman, Southern California Edison regional manager; Don Estes, owner of Salon de Ested; Kay Truesdale of the Sequoia and Kings National Parks Foundation; Reyes Zaragoza, Visalia Emergency Aid executive director, and Dennis Kemp, Voltage Multipliers president.

Oplinger will replace Stenger, who has been the interim executive director since April 1. Stenger, who has accepted a job as the women's ministry director at a local church, became interim director following the departure of Executive Director Maureen Chambers.

Linda Douglass, chairwoman of the Visalia

See Chamber/2A

Sales tax plan put on hold

By Matthew A. De Bellis
Times-Delta

Visalia Mayor Wally Gregory tested the political waters for a city sales tax at Monday night's City Council meeting, but opposition has stalled the plan for now.

He said he'd been feeling the heat from some fellow conservatives around town after talking about upping the city sales tax a quarter-cent to raise $3.1 million to hire more police officers. A half-cent countywide sales tax expires Dec. 31.

Gregory

"If you want more parks and youth facilities, somebody has to pay," Gregory said.

He proposed that 65 percent of the money raised would go to the Visalia police and fire departments, $500,000 to youth facilities, $300,000 for parks, $200,000 for park maintenance and $100,000 for city youth groups.

Gregory asked the four other council members to support and authorize his request to seek the support of state lawmakers.

Council members Evan Long and Don Landers supported the proposal. Landers said a sales tax is the most affordable option for the public.

Council members Jim Harbottle and Jesus Gamboa opposed the move.

"I am philosophically opposed to adding burdensome taxation to those we represent," Harbottle said in a prepared statement. "You can count me out."

Gamboa said he opposed moving toward a city tax because he had seen no analysis of what the Police Department and other community agencies need.

"If we put a price tag on it, I'd feel more comfortable," Gamboa said.

Gregory said he wouldn't proceed with any tax discussions or motions without the council members' full support.

"At this point now I will not go any further with this," he said. "I respect the council's comments."

Afterward, Gregory said he didn't feel rebuffed.

He said he will introduce a general advisory committee of about 20 residents from private industry, including farmers, bankers, teachers and attorneys at the Jan. 5 meeting.

The committee will advise council members on a variety of issues, including the possibility of a sales tax.

Steroids seized; 1 arrested

The goods — This picture, provided by the Visalia Police Department, shows some of the steroids seized Monday.

By Eric Coyne
Times-Delta

Undercover narcotics agents swooped down on an east Visalia gym Monday morning, arresting the owner on suspicion of the sale and possession of steroids.

Sgt. Steve Abbott said Visalia police searched the premises at Optimum Training Techniques, 546 S. Lovers Lane, and took proprietor [illegible] into custody.

Officers also seized two large boxes of paper receipts, invoices and sales records Abbott believes will help authorities track down the source of the drugs [illegible] allegedly obtained and sold to others.

"We've been checking up on this for three months now. We were following up on some complaints," Abbott said as he carried evidence out of the OTT gym.

Detective David Jarrett, the undercover officer who cracked the case, said when [illegible] was arrested, he had several prescriptions for steroids in his possession, including testosterone, a male hormone.

"We want to talk to the prescribing doctors and find out why he had these [prescriptions]," Jarrett said, then opened a bag and pulled out handfuls of hypodermic syringes he suspects the bodybuilder ordered from veterinary supply catalogs. "And something doesn't add up here. If he has all these steroids in pill form, why does he have all these needles?"

Jarrett would not elaborate on the circumstances, but said this wasn't the first time authorities had confronted [illegible] regarding the reported use and sale of steroids. Jarrett said that authorities earlier discovered a combination of steroids in both injectable liquid and pill form.

"[illegible] knew we were looking at him," Abbott said.

Also seized Monday during a search of [illegible] gym were several boxes of unidentifiable drugs and videotapes, including one labeled "The Anabolic Diet," that authorities said were advertised by Optimum Training Techniques. Jarrett said authorities believe it is a training tape showing how steroids can be used.

Officials would not say what the seized drugs were worth, but Jarrett indicated their value is "in the thousands."

Abbott said officials will now begin backtracking through [illegible] sales records to determine who he got the steroids from, and will continue interviewing several unnamed witnesses.

[illegible] arrest caught several customers by surprise, including a Visalia man who arrived at noon to work out but was turned away by narcotics officers.

"That's too bad," said the man, who declined to give his name. "[illegible] has two great kids."

[illegible] was taken to the Visalia Police Department Monday morning, booked by authorities and later transferred to the Bob Wiley detention center. He was being held in lieu of $20,000 bail.

[illegible] 42, a former Mt. Whitney High School quarterback, won the National Amateur Body Building Association heavyweight championship in 1995 and qualified to enter the Mr. Universe contest in London that year.

Tim Clapp, owner of Valley's Gym on East Main Street, said all too often professional bodybuilders use steroids to "bulk up" for competition, despite the risk of severe side effects and permanent health damage.

"It's not worth the risk," Clapp said. "There's no magic pill to lose weight or get in shape. It takes commitment and hard work."

Under arrest — [illegible], owner of Optimum Training Techniques, is escorted after booking at Visalia Police Department on suspicion of sales of illegal steroids.

Seeking reader input

What steps do Visalia-area athletes and bodybuilders take to add muscle, for personal or competitive reasons?

If you have direct experience or know someone who does, call the Times-Delta city desk at 735-3270 between 9 a.m. and 2 p.m. today.

Little League wins a round

Judge: Equipment should be kept by group, pending trial

By John Andrews
Times-Delta

Visalia Little League won a battle Monday in its legal war with Visalia Youth Baseball.

A judge awarded the group $42,500 in equipment and assets, pending a trial to settle the overall dispute.

Tulare County Superior Court Judge Howard Broadman issued a writ of possession, which gives Little League assets that have been held by Visalia Youth Baseball, formerly South Visalia American Little League.

Baseball equipment, uniforms, maintenance equipment, snack bar inventory and a bank account are included in the assets.

American Little League President Greg Riddle said Monday's ruling bodes well for his group.

"It's a dramatic move for a judge to take property from one side and give it to another," Riddle said. "A judge would only take this action if he felt our claim was substantial and we were likely to prevail."

Visalia Youth Baseball officials argued, however, that Broadman's decision will not figure in the overall ruling on whether Little League has a contractual right to the equipment and facilities.

"It is a setback, but this still isn't over," acting Visalia Youth Baseball President Arnie Duarte said Monday morning. "The lawsuit is going to determine what takes place."

What's next

Visalia Youth Baseball must submit a written response by Dec. 26 to Visalia Little League's lawsuit to gain control of disputed assets and facilities.

See Baseball/2A

Weather/2A
Morning fog
Today's High/low: 55/38
Monday's High/low: 52/41

Lottery
Daily 3
6 0 1
Fantasy 5
5/9/12/20/23
Saturday's Super Lotto
3/8/31/33/45/50
Lottery Hot Line:
(800) 225-8669

Stocks/5B
Dow Jones
High: 7,967.71
Low: 7,838.30
Close: 7,922.59

READER INPUT SOUGHT

Planning a New Year's Eve party or gathering?

The Visalia Times-Delta is compiling a list for a guide to events for the last day (and night) of 1997. Fax your information to Choices Editor Lisa M. Hansen at 735-3399 or send it to 330 N. West St., 93291.

100 years ago in Tulare County

"Mrs. Karrie Murray is making preparations for a Christmas tree entertainment for the benefit of the poor children who would not otherwise be happy," the Daily Delta reported

Index

Business	4B
Calendar	2A
Classified	9B
Comics	7B
Crossword	9B
Deaths	4A
Lifestyle	6B
Local	3A
Movies	8B
Nation	6A
Opinion	10A
Sports	1B
State	4A
TV	8B
World	11A

© 1997, VISALIA NEWSPAPERS FOR HOME DELIVERY, CALL: 735-3300 VOLUME 136, ISSUE 149

Spirit, not letter, of 1st Amendment endorsed

The Associated Press

NEW YORK — Americans overwhelmingly support the idea of the First Amendment, but many are willing to chip away at it over such issues as flag burning and prayer in schools, according to a poll released by The Freedom Forum on Monday.

"Americans truly believe they believe in free speech," said Paul McMasters, First Amendment watchdog at The Freedom Forum, a foundation established in 1935 by publishing mogul Frank E. Gannett.

But about things the amendment was written to protect — "the speech of the radical, the rascal, even the revolting — we become unsure," McMasters said.

More than nine out of 10 respondents — 93 percent — told pollsters they would vote yes if the Constitution's guarantee of freedom of speech, press, religion and association were being ratified today.

At the same time, 49 percent would amend it to prohibit flag-burning, which courts have ruled to be a form of political speech, and 42 percent want to let communities decide about school prayer, a potential breach of the separation of church and state.

Seventy-nine percent agree that newspapers should be allowed to publish freely and without government interference. But 38 percent say newspapers now have too much freedom. 35 percent would stop the press from reporting government secrets and 44 percent would keep cameras out of courtrooms.

The figures are from a poll of 1,026 American adults taken July 17 to Aug. 1 by the Center for Survey Research and Analysis at the University of Connecticut. The sampling error was 3 percentage points.

Ninety percent of those polled said people should be allowed to express unpopular opinions — but then 75 percent said they would not allow public speech that might be offensive to racial groups, 53 percent are against displaying art that may offend, and 47 percent would not allow songs with distasteful lyrics.

The article of my arrest as front page news in the local newspaper Times Delta.

For months after my article came out, I began to track newspaper articles to observe how they were written, as well as to try to determine why the newspaper ran certain stories as front-page feature stories, such as mine, compared to the smaller articles on the back pages. One particular article caught my attention and spurred me to call the paper. This small article was buried on the back pages. The story was about a business in town that was busted for fronting as a car detail shop; however, drugs were being sold. When the police entered this business they found guns, drugs, small children, and their parents. The person I was talking to was one of the higher-ups at the newspaper who was responsible for article placement. I asked why this article was buried towards the back and mine, with wildly inaccurate information, was a front-page feature story. I got an answer that was surprising, however refreshing and honest, which made me understand how sometimes the real world works.

She told me that the small article buried in the back was not a story that was unique; guns, drugs, and kids were a pretty common occurrence. However, someone like myself who had been successful in business for fifteen years and was very visible during those years because I took out full-page advertising, received national exposure, and had celebrity status due to some of my famous clientele, all made me a high-profile figure, especially in my hometown. In a strange way, what she told me gave me perspective and some closure to this part of my life and helped me move on.

It was all about selling newspapers, even at the expense of inaccurate information and the assassination of one's character and business. It didn't matter if what was being printed or portrayed wasn't completely true, as long as there was a version and a perception of the truth. That's how the game was played. After that phone call, I never tracked articles again. I focused on rebuilding my reputation, my business, and my personal life. Over the next two years things managed to work themselves out, not necessarily how I thought they would, but nevertheless they did.

Professionally, I was still operating my personal training business, which was on the mend and starting to make a slow comeback. Interestingly, all of the challenges and adversity I had to overcome made me a smarter businessman. The result of the steroid allegations ended with my begrudgingly agreeing to plea to a no contest verdict. My attorney advised this, even though he explained that based on all the evidence the prosecution had against me, the case was weak at best. However, he said, even though there was no question I was innocent, nothing is ever guaranteed when you put your destiny in the hands of a jury. The trial could last weeks, if not months, and would give the media even more to report. This additional negative media attention wouldn't be good for my business or for my kids.

I took the plea because it was the lesser of two evils. It left a bad taste in my mouth knowing that a no contest plea gave the perception that I was guilty, when I wasn't. My attorney said taking a no contest plea was a way to compromise with the prosecution, which would deflect the fact they had a weak case and make their reason for pursuing this case in the first place warranted. That's how the game is played. Life isn't always fair, and that's the real truth here. I wore an ankle bracelet and did community service for two years and kept moving on with my life. My personal life was still in deep repair. My divorce court proceedings were now over, which left me owing my ex-wife a lot of money and having to pay child support for the kids until they were out of high school. I had a lot of digging out to do. I ended up living with my mom while I was licking my wounds and trying to get my life back on track.

I was basically in survival mode for the next three years. This was like a bad dream all over again. In Phase One, I had experienced some very exciting moments within my sports career, which turned sour on me and ended in bitter disappointment. Now, in the third phase of my life after having taken a second chance at doing what I loved more than life itself, I was getting hammered and humbled all at the same time. The difference now was unlike in Phase One, the impact on my life was much greater because it affected my family and my business. History repeated itself. Life seems to have its own cycle.

Once again, a defining moment was staring me in the face. Sometimes we feel like giving up, or at least giving in, which is how I felt; however, down deep in my gut I knew I wouldn't. Not my nature. Life is going to kick the crap out of us sometimes, and even knock us down. The important thing is that we get up off the mat and fight back. So I did, but first I just needed a little down time to regroup, lick my wounds, and come up with a new game plan to move forward. This is where I think being a lifelong athlete served me best.

Sports can teach and build character and develop mental toughness. I spent the next couple of years lying low, rebuilding my business, and dealing with the details of my divorce. I actually stopped training altogether, which was weird considering that prior to all this, I ate and slept bodybuilding. What was even stranger was that I went a whole year without doing any exercise whatsoever. It was almost as if I was rebelling. It didn't make any sense to rebel against something I loved. Our mind-sets can be so crazy at times.

For a year all I did was train clients, eat, and gain eighty pounds, and it wasn't good weight. One day I got a wake-up call. I walked by a parked car and saw my reflection in the window. For a split second, I didn't recognize myself. Unbelievably, it was me. Up to that moment, I didn't think I looked that bad. I was very wrong and obviously in major denial.

CHAPTER ELEVEN

Dig Deeper

When the going gets tough, the tough get going.

—Joseph P. Kennedy

The reflection I saw that day had a jarring effect and put me into a proactive mode. I started dieting but didn't do any training. Over the next 10 months, I dropped 80 pounds. Our minds and bodies have an amazing way of adapting to their environment, compensating, or even playing tricks on us. During the year I gained that weight, not only did I not realize I looked as bad as I did, but I thought I felt pretty darn good. Little did I know, until I dropped the 80 pounds, that I could feel 100 percent better. Losing that weight was a jump-start. I felt motivated to do something else in addition to my dieting, but I didn't know what that should be.

From the time I retired from the sport of bodybuilding at the age of 41 until the age of 52, I concentrated on my personal training business, developing a franchise concept for personal studios, and writing new training courses targeting niche markets. This period of my life turned out to be very creative. I learned how to work in a very different way, trusting a very intuitive state of mind known as percolating, which is a creation mode. It's a form of daydreaming, and it allows you to take any idea from a raw undeveloped form to a finished, polished product. In my case, it was writing new content and concepts with regard to training and nutrition.

I was really focused. For the first time, I didn't have a woman in my life other than a long-distance friendship with a girl who I had met eight years earlier in Germany. This was the first time I had really been single, besides a three-year relationship following my marriage, which eventually ended. It was odd to adjust to because I was so used to being with someone. I got married at the age of 25 and was now single at the age of 46. It was a huge adjustment.

The next year was a growing period. The fact that I was unattached gave me time to learn how to exist without a girlfriend or a wife. I got to a point where I was okay being alone, and I didn't need anyone to make me happy. Ironically, as soon as I got to this point, I received a phone call from Tina, the Dutch girl I met eight years prior in Germany at a FIBO Health Fair. Anybody and everybody who had to do with fitness was there: trainers, gym apparel retailers, supplement companies, and many more. I was there with Tom Platz, one of the top professional bodybuilders, promoting my recent bodybuilding training manual *Big Beyond Belief.* After being stuck behind my booth for hours, I decided to take a break and walk around to see the other exhibits.

I remember turning the corner and seeing a vision that stopped me in my tracks. Tina had such exotic lips, and her hair was pulled back tight just the way I liked. I was pretty amazed. She was working at a booth selling gym apparel and believe it or not, I was too intimidated to talk to her, so I kept on walking and went back to my booth. All day I could not stop thinking about her and finally said screw it. So I went back, introduced myself, and we immediately hit it off. Before I left, we had dinner as friends and got to know one another.

I felt an unexplainable connection, but it was a connection I couldn't pursue. A day later, I was back on a plane headed home. That was it. She became a distributor in Germany for my bodybuilding training courses, and we maintained contact for about seven years. Then, all of a sudden she disappeared. I thought she had moved away or perhaps gotten married, until one day when I was shooting a video in Arizona, I received a phone call. It was her! It was her! It was her!

That phone call with Tina confirmed the feelings we had felt the first time we met in Germany. It was an unusual attraction; however, the timing and our circumstances back then were much different. Within a couple of weeks, I was on a plane back to Europe. As I headed out the door to the airport, I told my mom she should go buy a dress for my upcoming wedding because I knew Tina was going to be my second wife. The look on my mom's face was priceless! Considering that Tina and I hadn't seen each other for eight years, with only occasional phone calls here and there, I had made a pretty outrageous prediction. I was there for four days when we immediately started developing a relationship. On the third day, out of the blue, I asked her if she had ever visited the United States. She answered no, so I asked her if she wanted to come visit for the holidays. She mentioned that she didn't have a valid passport and to take a week off from her busy schedule would be impossible. I then dropped to one knee and asked her to marry me. Surprisingly she said, "Yes, I let you go the first time, but never again." I'll never forget that.

The news shocked and surprised her family, as well as mine. Tina is one of 11 children, and I hadn't met any of her siblings. When she told her family she was getting married to a guy she had met eight years earlier at a health fair and was moving to America, her family was shocked, which was understandable. As far as my family, well, when I told them I was getting married again, they didn't believe me. Surprise, surprise.

It took three months to get Tina and her dog to America by plane and her furniture and belongings by ship. She landed December 22, 2002, in Los Angeles on a Saturday, and two days later we were married at the courthouse in my hometown. Two months later we put on a beautiful, intimate wedding at a country club and invited friends and family. Her oldest sister and best friend came from Europe to meet me and support her at the wedding.

Tina and I on our wedding day at the Visalia
Country Club in my hometown.

This was the second time around for both Tina and me. Tina was also married when she was younger. As I write this, we are going on our 12th year. Except for those first eight days together, our relationship was built on a long-distance friendship via telephone calls and letters. We really got to know each other's ways only after we got married and began our day-to-day life together. It's been an interesting journey, especially adapting to each other's cultural differences.

Tina is exactly what I needed in my life because she brought a fresh new perspective. I didn't realize how much the two years of divorce and fighting criminal charges beat me up until she came along. In a way it was like wiping the slate clean with new hopes and dreams, but the reality was that I still had a lot of mess to clean up.

It was nice to have somebody like Tina by my side. She knew what I had been through and was up for the challenges ahead. She immediately started coming up with ideas to potentially improve our personal training business. They were good ideas and ones that I'd thought of myself; however, I had not one ounce of energy to promote one other thing in my life during my time in survival mode. With someone like Tina in my court, who had the desire that I couldn't muster up, it felt like all things were possible.

The next few years were a steady trend of positive things happening. With Tina's help, I tripled the size of my personal training business. Life is always trying to teach us lessons that can be of benefit in our future; however, sometimes it's hard to understand how. During the time I was getting pounded with court battles and negative publicity it was very difficult to find the lesson I needed to learn. Time is a great teacher. The two years of hell that I went through taught me what I could endure, which surpassed anything I could have imagined. That dark time also taught me how to succeed in my personal training business when everything was against me. I had to learn every possible way to survive, which meant coming up with new ideas to generate income. The adversity and pain of what I went through was what I needed to expand my creative potential.

I developed other opportunities from my personal training business, which created additional streams of revenue without creating any extra overhead. The first was a certification program for individuals who wanted to become personal trainers. This was a perfect and natural way for me to leverage my own experience of what I had learned from training and nutrition and to share it with others.

The second was developing a turn-key business opportunity for other personal trainers wanting to establish their own personal training business, or even individuals who wanted to own their own business and have trainers working for them. With new hopes and dreams, my new wife and I ventured out. Over the next few years, I certified trainers and helped people get into their own business, which gave me satisfaction in addition to making some decent money. But something was missing. This wasn't punching all my buttons. I even thought that opening up a chain of my own personal training studios would quench my thirst, but that didn't happen, either.

In addition to all these new changes in my life, I had started to look for a new hobby as well. When I traveled to Germany I was amazed at how most of the people there were in excellent shape. It then occurred to me that most of them were riding bicycles, so when I got back I decided that, in addition to my dieting, I was going to start riding my bike. After about a month of riding to the gym I decided to take it to the next level. I became a fan of long-distance competitive cycling. Based on my naturally bigger body type, competitive bicycling was not really compatible, and yet I was pretty darn good at it.

Here is a picture of me at a double century cycling
competition on the Ride to Kaiser.

One thing I liked about long-distance cycling was it developed incredible endurance; however, I didn't like the way my body looked. I thought I looked skinny, and I don't look good skinny. I was used to having lots of muscle on my body, and I much preferred that look instead. Seeing me on a bike climbing steep grades was like solving the mystery of how a bumble bee with its big body and short wing span can fly. It defies the laws of physics. I competed for four years consistently, then just like I did with bodybuilding, from one day to the next, I stopped riding and haven't been on a bike since. I knew in my heart of hearts I was still chasing my childhood dream of being a pro athlete and I was falling short.

Bodybuilding, traveling the world, and training celebrities as well as achieving celebrity status came very close to recapturing that elusive dream, but it all came crashing down when the wheels fell off of my personal life. I've always been a dreamer with a determined personality, and I would continue to search for the magic in my life that would reignite that fire in the belly. After a 13-year retirement, I decided to go back to what made me feel good, which was bodybuilding. At the age of 53, I decided to compete again. Bodybuilding made me feel like I was back home. It was the closest thing to giving me the passion I felt when I was younger and chasing my childhood dream.

Once you have passion for something and it's gone, nothing else is ever good enough, and you're always left feeling that something is missing. That is too much pain to have to deal with. Life is too short.

Having bodybuilding back in my life the second time around was different and better than ever. The fire in my belly never burned any hotter and this time, because of the 13-year layoff, I had a different kind of appreciation for it. As the saying goes, you don't realize what you have until it's gone. I was once again alive inside. I had some lofty goals and couldn't wait to get started and achieve them. I had a three-year action plan, which was to get my body back into world-level condition to compete and win the Masters Men's Nationals in my age group.

To reach my goal, I would have to rely on hard work, muscle memory, and perfect willingness. The first three weeks back in the gym were a shock to say the least. I was 13 years older, and my joints didn't let me forget it. They screamed loud and clear and definitely got my attention.

It took six months before it felt like my body was going to be able to handle the abuse it would need to take to be competition ready. Being older, I would have to make some adjustments to get my body to respond, and I did. My return to the stage to compete was amazing. I was happy about the condition I achieved in my first year and knew that with two more years of consistent training, and barring any catastrophe, I would be at world- level condition.

I had one year of training under my belt. My off-season training program in year two had provided a platform for my body to explode in terms of packing on muscle at a rate that even in my younger days wasn't possible. This was evidence that the physiology had muscle memory, but it also told me that having all of the years of training gave me the experience and ability to make a stronger mind and muscle connection, which dramatically accelerated exercise performance. I was in such a focused state that it felt like being in a trance.

About seven months into my off-season training, I weighed 300 pounds and was getting ready for the biggest amateur event I could possibly compete in. My body wanted more.

At this point, I had two personal training studios in operation, which were in two different towns about 10 miles apart. It was a stressful time running two studios. I was working 15 hours a day, in addition to training like a wild man. I became possessed by the extreme behavior that the sport of bodybuilding can produce. I was sleeping only three to four hours a day. All of this extreme behavior put my body in adrenaline overload, and it was a recipe for disaster. In fact my body did try to warn me, but I was so focused on my upcoming competition that I ignored the first sign of trouble.

After one of my morning training sessions, I passed out in the back of my truck outside the studio. I had put the tailgate down to sit and take a rest. I remember I was unusually exhausted after this particular workout and just wanted to get some fresh air and sit down. After a few minutes resting on my tailgate, I felt a sensation of calm and peacefulness, then I started slipping away. It felt very different than any other sensation I had ever felt. I was aware on some level what was happening, but I didn't care: It was peaceful.

A client who was leaving the studio saw me laid out and noticed I didn't respond after she said goodbye a few times. She came over to check on me, and then she realized I was passed out. Fortunately, she intuitively thought to get some yogurt from the studio refrigerator. With the help of another client, she sat me up on my tailgate and helped me become coherent enough to eat yogurt, which slowly brought me back to being alert. They called 911. Shortly after the ambulance arrived, the paramedics quickly determined that my blood sugar was dangerously low. They gave me an IV at my studio and suggested I go to the hospital to get checked out, but I stubbornly refused and didn't go.

Business went on as usual. The following day, once again after my morning training session, I had a similar experience, except this time I was driving to get a haircut and started feeling like the lights were going dim and my vision was becoming blurred to an extent I almost couldn't see. This really scared me.

Fortunately, I was close enough to a Jack in the Box restaurant, so I pulled in the drive-thru to place an order, barely hanging on to consciousness. Even in this condition my survival instincts kicked in. I ordered a rice bowl because I knew that if I had low blood sugar, the rice with its high starch content would bring me back to a coherent state, and it did.

This was yet another warning my body was sending me, and yet I still didn't go to the doctor. Through my own research I determined what was happening to me was called adrenal burnout. This was a direct result of my mind and body being so stressed out and pushed too close to the edge of collapsing. My adrenal glands were over-stimulated to their maximum capacity and had completely shut down. I was about five months out from being competition ready, and there was nothing that would keep me from competing. I carried on even after these two warning shots fired by my body. The combination of being completely consumed by bodybuilding and having perfect willingness would not allow me to be objective enough to realize the thin ice I was on in terms of my health. For me, it's always been about risk and reward and sometimes you have to roll the dice. It's a part of my nature to be a gambler, and it's been an ongoing personality trait throughout my life. I was going to compete.

I made some adjustments in my personal life and pre-contest preparation to address my adrenal burnout issue. My adjustments seemed to be working, and my training seemed to be back on track. There was no more passing out, and I felt pretty good, all things considered. There is no getting around the extreme behavior that comes with the sport of bodybuilding, so we just learn to tolerate the suffering. As more time went on, I was confident I had overcome my adrenal burnout. I was now two months away from the biggest competition of my bodybuilding career. That's when the unthinkable happened.

Posing at the Men's Nationals (master division) at the age of 55. This was the last competition before I had my strokes.

CHAPTER TWELVE

Getting Bucked Off the Horse

The difference between who you are, and who you want to be, is what you do.

—Bill Phillips, *Body for Life*

I had three strokes in three weeks and was now paralyzed. My world as I knew it had come to a screeching halt. I went from being in complete control of every muscle in my body, to not having any control at all. I felt disconnected, empty, and scared of the future. Having one stroke was devastating enough, let alone three. As I lay in my hospital bed paralyzed for the third time, I knew this time was different. With my previous strokes I wasn't scared, and I believed I could overcome and tough it out. Lying in that hospital bed for seven days after having my third stroke was the longest week of my life. So many thoughts and emotions were coursing through my mind and body. To say it was overwhelming doesn't come close to expressing the devastation that I felt.

I was now terrified of what was to come. My life was continuously flashing before me. I questioned everything. How did I get here? Why did this awful thing happen to me? How could this happen to someone who had been active, in shape, and an athlete for most of his life? I had been involved in the personal fitness training business for more than 30 years; I had helped and trained thousands of clients at my studios, all in the pursuit of achieving specific goals related to nutrition and exercise. In addition, I had been a competitive athlete since the age of eight, and was still competing at the national and world level into my mid 50s in bodybuilding competitions. I didn't understand it and I knew there was a good chance I never would.

I then started thinking about my future. When something life changing happens to us we instantly think why and then realize the biggest concern we have to face is the future and what it has in store for us. I didn't know how this would impact my life, my wife, and my children. Could I possibly recover fully and be the man I once was after three major setbacks like these? And in such a short period of time? Even though I had doctors, nurses, family, and friends as a support group, I had never felt so alone. There was so much at stake and I felt helpless, which I was at that very moment. I was living the biggest nightmare of my life, uncertain of my future and whether or not I'd ever fully recover. Everything gets put into perspective in a heartbeat when your back is against a wall and you feel like you're fighting for your life.

After day three I decided I was going to get out of bed with no assistance from the nurse and use the restroom, which was only a few feet away. I took two steps and crashed into the wall, almost falling to the floor. I didn't have the control I needed to walk. From that point forward, I was somewhat afraid to walk alone. This fact shook my confidence at the deepest level. When you can't do the most basic thing you have been doing since you were a baby, like walking, it scares the hell out of you and causes gut-wrenching frustration. I felt helpless. What a turn of events for someone who was used to being able to control literally every muscle in his body. Now I needed assistance to walk just a few feet.

A few days before I was scheduled to be released from the hospital, I had a physical and speech therapist come to see me and show me some very basic things I could do at home as a form of physical therapy. Additionally, the doctor had prescribed outpatient physical therapy for more extensive sessions. I had two weeks before my rehab therapy would start. In the meantime, doing very basic things at home was the beginning of my therapy. It was unbelievable. I needed help with everything. But my mind-set, attitude, and fighting spirit had started to improve since leaving the hospital. I knew I was in a dogfight, and it was either all or nothing.

As the doctor prescribed, I went to my first and what would be my last physical therapy session. The physical therapist had no idea about my experience as a bodybuilder. She didn't ask about my background, nor did I emphasize it. My instincts told me that based on our conversation, and what I perceived, the physical therapist's expectations didn't match mine. I felt like her goal was to get me to a place where I could be functional, doing the basic things. My goal, however, was a full recovery. The fact that I came to this conclusion in just one session might have been unfair to her, but I believed that with my bodybuilding and athletic background, I could do better.

I was definitely at a crossroads. I knew I had to make an important decision and commitment to my full recovery because anything less was not an option. Even though I was advised by my doc that I should give up the sport of bodybuilding, I knew in order to overcome the biggest hurdle of my life, I would have to attack my recovery process with the same mind-set and mental tenacity it took to pack on muscle.

As hard as it sometimes was to train as a bodybuilder, suffering through the grueling workouts, it was child's play compared to the effort it would take to reconnect my mind to the right side of my impaired body, which was now scrambled and disconnected. I'm convinced this is where bodybuilding really saved my life. I could use the experience from all of the years of training and thousands of reps, implementing and executing techniques like perfecting the mind and muscle connection, to produce dramatic results. This was exactly what

I needed at this very crucial, make-or-break period of my life. I knew I had to come up with my own training strategy for creating my own rehab recovery. I was confident in my ability and could draw on my years of bodybuilding experience to be successful. I had no doubt I could do this. It was time to redefine my potential and reinvent myself.

CHAPTER THIRTEEN

Reinventing My Potential

Rock bottom became the solid foundation on which I rebuilt my life.

—J.K. Rowling, 2008 Harvard
University Commencement

There is usually something positive that comes out of a negative occurrence if you're willing to make lemonade out of lemons. I took off four and a half months to recover and rehabilitate myself. I learned how unbelievably amazing and powerful the mind and body is and what it's capable of adapting to if you have perfect willingness.

In conjunction with my home training rehab, I had to come up with a game-plan strategy to be able to deal with the inevitable questions I'd have to address sooner or later from my personal training clients as to why I wasn't at my studio.

Unlike with my first two strokes, where no one knew that anything happened since I was back at work the following week, this time would be very different considering it would be four and a half months before my return.

I didn't want any of my clients to see me like this, or for that matter anyone. I was embarrassed, too vain, and concerned about how my strokes would impact my business. My son Josh and wife Tina were working in the studio at the time when all of this went down and would initially end up having to answer questions as to my whereabouts. They both trained my clients, and I was like the Wizard of Oz behind the curtain, pulling the strings to generate clients and keep money flowing in. I did consultations over the phone, promoted the business, and addressed any issues that clients had because they didn't see me around the gym. I told Tina and Josh not to say anything about my strokes, and I would do the same. When it did come up, we admitted something happened but made up a story instead of telling the truth. I knew I put them in a tough spot because I was asking them not to tell the whole truth.

Eventually I knew people would find out, but in my mind I rationalized they didn't need to know for sure until I was ready to tell them myself. This was personal, and I would keep it that way as long as necessary. I suspected clients might be concerned whether or not the studio would remain open, and that was always the intention. I'm very pleased to announce that it is still open today.

This would be my strategy and the story I would stick to no matter what. I even went as far as not admitting to people who knew for sure, or so they thought. I did admit something had happened, but I never admitted to the strokes. I was too embarrassed and ashamed.

How could someone like me, who was in the fitness business training and teaching people how to get in shape and be healthy, still have any credibility? Now that time has passed, and I have a whole new perspective, I've learned I probably could have been more forthcoming about what happened. Having a strong team of close special friends and family around helped me through a tough time and was very invaluable to me. My personal training business would have never made it if not for my son, wife, and loyal clients. I thank them for that.

As far as my day-to-day therapy, I knew first and foremost I had to understand at a deeper level just exactly what I was up against. I needed to do some research, so I proceeded to learn facts about what causes strokes, how many strokes happen every year, the percentage of people who have 100 percent recovery, and what general stroke protocol is.

I would start by practicing my walking, which is considered a gross motor skill and generally recovers sooner than the fine motor skills such as speech. At this point I was impaired. My right arm and hand had the most damage and had little or no movement. My speech was slurred, and the right side of my face was paralyzed. My right leg was the least affected. However, I would have to overcome paralysis in the lower leg, which caused a drag and a noticeable limp when I walked.

I would practice my walk inside my house and around the back-yard. I didn't want anyone to see me rehabbing, at least not yet. To a degree, I would apply what I learned from my training in bodybuild-ing, such as repetition being the mother of skill, and know that my body would become its function. In essence, I had to teach my body specifically what I wanted it to do and how I wanted it to respond.

It's odd and very difficult to put so much attention and effort into something as basic as learning how to walk properly again. I know without a doubt if I didn't have the experience and training from body-building, it would have been so much more of a challenge. In fact, I can really understand now why people sometimes give up. Having a stroke beats you up, down, and sideways every day.

After a month of walking inside my house and around my back-yard, I decided to take my walking out on my street. In my mind, this was the next step in terms of advancing my recovery. The fact that I might be seen by some neighbors stressed me out because I knew I wasn't walking properly. In my little mind it bothered me if they could tell. I was too vain for my own good.

This was an issue I had to overcome. Otherwise I could see myself withdrawing, which would not help me accomplish my objective of a full recovery. I created a proactive action strategy to get me out in public to further my progress. I called it PIP (Practice in Public).

I started practicing at a couple of places where I felt comfortable, and I went for it. I'll admit I was nervous, but like most anything you do practicing helps you get better, and the more I got out and practiced, the more comfortable I became. I learned to face my fear and perform with confidence. Our minds are such powerful tools once we learn how to harness our thoughts.

Amazingly, I never realized when I was walking how uneven surfaces are even though they look smooth. We take for granted all of the adjustments the brain and body make seamlessly and on the fly to eliminate thinking about every move we make.

Learning how to walk again as well as I once did would require me to create new pathways in my brain by developing a stronger link between my brain and the body part that was being targeted. Here's some good news! What has been discovered since the 1960s is that our brain has the ability to build brand-new pathways, bypassing the damaged parts caused by stroke.

Developing a stronger link between the brain and the muscle was exactly the same thing I did when I trained for bodybuilding. The real difference between these two examples is that prior to my strokes, the pathways to my brain were open. Post-stroke, the area in my brain where the strokes occurred was permanently damaged and closed forever.

Here's even better news: not only can our brains build new pathways, but starting rehab sooner increases stroke rehab results and lengthens recovery time dramatically. In fact as I write this, I'm still receiving results on a regular basis, even at 30 months after my third stroke. Before 1960, the popular opinion in the medical field was that most of the results received could only occur within the first six months after a stroke.

Our bodies are capable of more than we think. However, it takes consistent persistence and belief. I learned so much from bodybuilding that I've applied to my stroke recovery. In bodybuilding, for example, you have to constantly look for new exercises or perfect existing exercises to create ongoing results.

Some exercises and little tricks I discovered and stumbled upon that helped improve results for my impaired leg included standing on a foam pad, which improved stability and balance, especially when I stood on one leg or stood on the pad while closing my eyes. Another one was walking while wearing sandals. I noticed that when I walked, my left sandal would make a flip noise when it hit my heel, but this didn't happen with my right heel because my calf had paralysis. So I started focusing on making the right sandal flip. This trick fired my calf muscles.

Walking backward improved what's called "drop foot," which is a neurological issue caused by damage to the nerve in the leg. Another trick was as simple as changing shoes on a regular basis, which forces your brain and body to adapt to subtle differences. Last but not least, since I began my physical therapy training 30 months ago, I've never missed a workout.

Bringing my right arm and hand back to full recovery would be a bigger hill to climb. This part of my body was the most impacted, and it had a greater degree of fine motor skill that would have to be developed. It would be like starting over. In a sense, I was like a newborn baby who was unaware of his body, with little or no connection from brain to muscle. I couldn't get my brain to signal any of the muscles in my right arm or hand to contract. I was now an adult fully aware of how disconnected I was from my right arm and hand. It was devastating not to be able to do something as easy as feeding myself.

Twenty years of bodybuilding taught me how valuable it was to connect the mind to the muscle for more efficient results. I had to teach my body what I wanted it to do using the same mind-set and focus when I was a bodybuilder. My immediate and specific objective would be to do a biceps curl where I would raise my hand from down at my side to the front of my shoulder.

Initially I had to have my wife help me raise my hand through that range of motion several times. I would watch intently, looking at the muscle and visualizing that I was doing the exercise on my own. The purpose of this was to let my eyes see my arm successfully do the curl and mentally send the message to my brain, which in turn would pass the message to the biceps muscle. After doing this for two weeks, eventually the connection was made, and I was able to do the curling motion on my own.

The most powerful tool in the world is thought. This is clearly shown in the example of how, after two weeks, my brain made the physiological connection to the muscle through repetition. There was nothing in my 20 years of intense training as a bodybuilder that was harder than trying to teach my arm and hand to move again. Our body's ability to adapt to its environment is truly amazing, but in order to maximize the true benefit we have to be willing to put in the time and effort. When our objective is to fully recover from a stroke, we have to be tenacious. It's a marathon, not a sprint, to the finish line.

I have now spent 30 months of rehab training for my arm and hand, and the results have been astonishing. Progress continues on a regular basis. My instincts told me that because of the high degree of fine motor skill the arm and hand possess, by its physiological nature, it would take more frequent training sessions to maximize the full potential of recovery.

One day out of the blue, it occurred to me that I had so many more options available that I could incorporate into my rehab training for my arm and hand. It was so obvious, and right in front of me, yet I had missed it. I realized I could get the benefits from everyday tasks I performed: twisting caps on and off bottles, turning doorknobs, and hanging up hangers. However, I would make them more productive by changing my focus when I performed them. Now I was able to do effective rehab every day, essentially all day, focusing on the movements I wanted to get back so I could perform them as I once had.

Thinking about how I was performing these everyday tasks improved my results dramatically. I developed the ability through bodybuilding to efficiently train the muscle, strengthening the mind and muscle connection. I developed a mantra, which helped maintain my laser beam focus: "Do what you do every day."

One very valuable trick I learned to accelerate results was mirror therapy. Mirror therapy is a specific therapy designed to strengthen arms and hands weakened by a stroke. In mirror therapy, we use the movements of the stronger hand and arm to trick our brain into thinking that the weaker arm is moving. Researchers have shown that this "tricking of the brain" actually works. I would put a squeezable ball in both hands and while sitting on a chair, place a long mirror between my legs. The mirror would be facing my left hand and hiding my impaired one. I would squeeze the ball in my left hand only, really focusing on the movement. I could feel the delay between my mind and the muscle connection in my right hand. I was skeptical but hopeful. Then after about two weeks, my right hand could squeeze the ball again. The brain areas that were responsible for making my weaker arm move had become stimulated. It was the weirdest feeling, but a good one. In a matter of weeks, the body part that was paralyzed was now working!

It's hard to believe that using a mirror could trick the brain like this. If not for having firsthand experience, I don't know if I would have believed it either. When you want to improve you have to be willing to push the envelope, to experiment and hope for the best.

CHAPTER FOURTEEN

Let's Talk

*F-E-A-R has two meanings: Forget Everything and
Run or Face Everything and Rise.*

—Zig Ziglar

Now it was time to get my speech back. My stroke left me with
paralysis on the right side of my mouth and my tongue. This caused
a slur in my speech. I discovered I couldn't say certain words or even
whistle. I would have to train my tongue to learn all over again.

I also had developed a bit of a stutter, which I never had before.
My strategy for recovery would be to follow the same protocol I implemented for my leg, arm, and hand. Repetition being the mother of
skill, and the body becoming its function, would be the rehab training
methodology of choice. Simply put, I would speak so that my tongue

would learn once again how to form the correct shapes to say the words. It was easier said than done.

When we are self-conscious about our impairments, and I was, there is a tendency to withdraw and not want to talk. In order to get better we have to be willing to make mistakes. I knew I had to push on. To help improve and accelerate my speech recovery I spoke a foreign language and sang my ABCs out loud. Speaking in a language other than my own was a specific exercise that forced my brain and tongue to adapt. I practiced in my family's native Portuguese, which taught me to roll my R's again. This translated into results. Singing my ABCs out loud helped with the articulation of each specific letter. Just like my rehab training for my leg, I implemented PIP (Practice in Public). Every day, I would practice privately the words with which I struggled. Then I would go out in public and practice on strangers.

Overcoming adversity requires getting out of our comfort zone. When I was in my thirties one of my fears was public speaking. I found it much harder to speak in front of people I knew, rather than to strangers, but I overcame it.

My speech impediment caused me anxiety and embarrassment. It affected my confidence. I cared much less if strangers could tell, as opposed to people I knew. So I applied what I learned from overcoming public speaking and initially practiced learning how to get my speech back with strangers. I spoke with individuals who worked in technical support and talked on the phone with other people. They didn't know who I was and couldn't see me. Some results were fairly immediate, but most of the changes happened within three weeks. This gave me confidence.

Life wants to keep teaching us lessons, and what I learned from getting my speech back was that it all starts in the mind. As I learned through repetition to effectively control my emotions during stressful situations, my confidence and my ability to overcome my speech impediment improved dramatically. Now I can talk to anyone!

CHAPTER FIFTEEN

Move Forward, Move On

To evolve is to be a better version of yourself.

—Leo Costa, Jr.

The first four and a half months after my strokes were one giant learning curve. Unlike bodybuilding, the training protocol for my stroke therapy felt like uncharted water. As I was figuring out what I needed to do for my stroke therapy, I learned there were many bodybuilding techniques I could incorporate. After months of home therapy, I was now at a point where I needed to take another big step in order to push my recovery to the next level.

I would go back to my personal training studio to face clients who hadn't seen me in four and a half months. I was nervous because I wasn't 100 percent recovered, but I felt it was time to start training with weights in a very conservative fitness program. In order to keep making progress, we have to challenge ourselves and sometimes do things that scare us. We have to manage to work through our fear to keep moving forward. As I said, I was nervous about being around my clients because I was less than 100 percent recovered, which made me feel insecure.

Quite a few knew something had happened, but they weren't sure exactly what it was. Some could tell my arm and hand weren't quite right. This is an example of challenging ourselves and overcoming our fears. I instinctively knew if I didn't face the music now it would just get harder, so I bit the bullet.

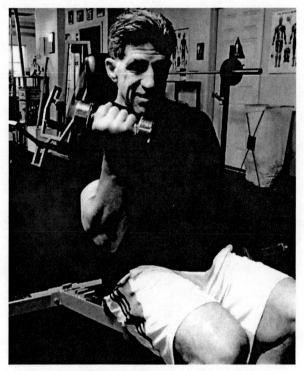

A year after my strokes I was able to do an
unassisted curl with 5 pounds.

When I competed in the sport of bodybuilding it was all about getting up on stage and displaying my physique in its best light. This meant showing the audience what I wanted them to see, and hiding what I didn't want them to see. It's amazing how the things I've learned from my bodybuilding career applied to my life post-stroke.

I would apply what I learned from being up on the stage of a bodybuilding competition to the stage of life. When I trained in my personal training studio, it became my stage and my clients the audience. I would show them what I wanted them to see. I made it a point to be aware of my body in space. I would become a master of disguise. I became very effective at minimizing my impairment, while also making progress in my recovery. To disguise my impairment even further, I made it a point to pay attention to detail and created even more distraction with a complete makeover. In four and a half months of being away from the studio, I had dropped 40 pounds. I also created a whole new look with a different hairstyle. My strategy worked as intended; my new look got a lot of attention. I love when a plan comes together.

Here I am a year after my strokes doing an
unassisted chest press with 45 pounds.

What I had done was develop a successful formula. I became productive with my rehab therapy without feeling self-conscious about my body not being 100 percent, while improving and staying on my mission for full recovery. But there was still some confidence building and emotional issues I needed to deal with in other areas of my life to make a full, well-rounded recovery.

In bodybuilding one of the lessons that came with the sport was how difficult it was to add muscle to the body. We always talked about it being a marathon, not a sprint. In some cases it could take years of dedicated persistent training to get the desired results. This lesson served me well in my stroke recovery considering it took two years of day-to-day practice to be able to grab a fork from the table with my impaired hand to feed myself. The real message here is to never ever, ever, ever give up because your next breakthrough is just around the corner. When this happens you'll feel an incredible sense of accomplishment. It's euphoric.

Once when I got bucked off a horse, my dad told me to get back on sooner than later because if I waited too long, negative thoughts, loss of confidence, and fear could set in. If you have fear when you ride a horse, the animal can sense it and is more likely to buck you off. My strokes essentially bucked me off my life as I knew it. I was now a different person in some ways and never as emotional as I was at this point in my life. For the first six months after my strokes, it wasn't unusual for me to start crying or laughing uncontrollably for no apparent reason. This made me feel vulnerable and out of control. As I write this it's been thirty months, and I still have moments when I get blindsided by emotion.

I knew I needed to get back to doing some of the things I did prior to my strokes before too much time had passed. I had to get back on that horse to help get my confidence back. I decided I could do this by making business trips to Los Angeles and San Francisco while driving alone in my car, as well as making public appearances and presentations. But in the back of my mind, I had doubt.

I remember the first time I drove to San Francisco. Most of the drive was fine. However, dealing with the stress of driving in fast traffic made me anxious. At times during the drive, I had panicky thoughts about what I would do if I had another stroke in the middle of traffic. I realized that I didn't know where a hospital was located. The thought of that possibility was scary, and yet I had to have a plan in case it happened. I had to manage the adversity and my fear and continue on.

At this exact moment, I felt raw fear about being 200 miles away from home alone, and only four and a half months out from having three strokes. My mind was racing and in a state of panic. When our minds are out of control, it can make us think and feel so many things. At times we don't even know what is actually happening or even what is true.

In this chaotic moment, I learned something about myself that I might not have discovered had I not decided to make this trip. I learned how to perform effectively when I felt gut-wrenching anxiety and fear. I had to put myself in a state of thinking that I was okay. So I controlled my fear and forced myself to focus on anything else but the worst-case scenario. I thought about what was directly in front of me and never lost track of my destination. In this instance, I was able to harness my state of panic and anxiety, making it work for and not against me.

I can't tell you how amazing and relieved I felt when I made it to San Francisco. I broke down in tears. I'm even overwhelmed with emotion as I'm writing this. Needless to say, my confidence level grew immediately. That initial trip to San Francisco was a stepping stone to helping me get my life back. When we have a strategy to be proactive, a goal and a desire to implement out of that planning will create a reproducible formula for success in other areas, as it did when I began making public appearances again.

Recovery from a stroke puts everything into perspective. It's like taking baby steps. It's going to take quite some time to get from point A to point B. The results for me never came as fast as I wanted, but they came, and they're still coming. I'm good with that.

I wouldn't wish a stroke on anyone, but in my case, I consider myself fortunate. Although my three strokes were bad enough to cause severe impairment, ultimately I was able to overcome and recover. Through this process of recovery and rediscovery, I learned a lot about my spirit and commitment to fight what at times seemed to be insurmountable odds. The challenge was like a mountain too steep to scale, and yet I somehow was able to do it.

I've mentioned that life wants to teach us lessons even when we're unaware. Bodybuilding taught me valuable things such as persistence through the repetition of consistency and made me highly aware and in tune with my mind and body. I applied this information in my stroke recovery, which accelerated dramatic results.

Three years after my strokes I was able to
curl 35 pounds, unassisted!

This is me three years after my strokes doing a bench
press and now bench pressing175 pounds!

Having three strokes was devastating, no question, but because of
the strokes, I was forced to search deep inside myself to find the lesson
life was trying to teach me, and I did. Strangely, what appeared to be
something negative had become just the opposite. With that, brand-
new possibilities and exciting opportunities have presented themselves
and in many ways made me better than ever.

I've become a better trainer because I now understand even more
and at a much deeper level what the mind and body are capable of.
In bodybuilding, you learn about mind and muscle connection. It
becomes something that is drilled into your mind. You practice it and
believe in good faith and by trial and error, it will work. I had experienced the mind and muscle connection on a whole different level and
with a whole different perspective. This is how bodybuilding helped
me with my recovery. I went from having no connection, to connecting my body to my mind once again. This just backed up everything I
was ever taught. Through this discovery I am able to communicate and
teach my clients at a more effective level. Finally, the adversity I've had

to overcome drove and enlightened me to a new awareness of my capabilities. It gave me a new vision and outlook so that I could reinvent the potential of my life.

I've learned how to manage and channel the part of my personality that has a tendency to be addicted to extreme behavior and make it productive rather than destructive. So out of a major setback in my life came some major breakthroughs. As odd as this may sound, like my experience with bodybuilding, having three strokes saved my life.

If I didn't have the perfect willingness I learned from bodybuilding, which took twelve years, I know for a fact I wouldn't be where I am today in my recovery. I was used to intense training to create a physique that was good enough to compete at the world level. The sad truth, as I've learned from my own firsthand experience, is so many people have compromised their potential for full recovery because they gave up too soon. I totally understand what they felt because of my own journey back. There were times I was so frustrated because I wanted to make my body do something so simple, like feed myself, and I couldn't. That can kill a person's spirit.

Thirty months after my stroke I am more grateful than ever and proud to report that my recovery has been very successful. It's because of the bodybuilding mind-set strategy I implemented, including nontraditional techniques and treatments. It has given my brain and body the ability to continue to recover and become even better than I was prior to my strokes.

CHAPTER SIXTEEN

It's a Matter of Thought

What defines us is how well we rise after falling.

—*Maid in Manhattan* (2002)

When bad things happen to people, there are usually two ways they can respond. Some, because of the adversity, are defined by it, but they excel to become better than they were. And some are devastated by the adversity to the point that it destroys their life. Life will either make or break you. There are no shortages of tests in this life. I was being tested. I didn't like it, but that didn't matter. It's just the way life works. Lying in that bed, a part of me felt everything, and yet I was completely disconnected from my body.

When I look back in hindsight, I realize that throughout my life there has been a time and place for everything, with its own rhythm and tempo. This has challenged me in ways I could have never anticipated. Now, being in the present phase of my life, I can clearly see new possibilities for my future. I have learned things from my life that have helped me understand how I've gotten to where I am today. It's definitely been an interesting journey.

My perception and my reality now reveal that life has been testing me. In fact it's been a series of tests, some with no answers as to why, at least not at the time. I find the concept of time very powerful in how fast and slow it goes, and one of the lessons I learned from time slowing down was that it was trying to prepare me for what I had to do to fully recover. Forty-three months ago I went to great lengths to make sure no one knew I had three strokes, and now I'm at a place where I want to share my experience openly, which has been cathartic. Again, I wouldn't want what happened to me to happen to anyone else, but the hard fact and reality is in the United States alone, it happens to about 800,000 people a year. Strokes can be devastating, as well as preventable. However, it is possible to fully recover from a stroke if you're informed and armed with the tools necessary to dramatically increase results.

I'm still making progress on a regular basis, which is a testimonial to the training strategy and approach I've developed and followed. We never really know what's possible until we try, and I urge everyone to try. Part of my reason for writing this book was for self-discovery and to learn how the choices and paths I took impacted my life's journey, and this has led me to learn that even though I've gone through moments in my life when I felt frustrated and sorry for myself, asking "Why me?" was the wrong question to ask. I realize now I have been fortunate. As crazy as it seems (and it feels even crazier to write this), the experience of having three strokes has become one of the best things that's happened to me.

I sincerely hope that my life journey can inspire and help others. My mission now is to continue to educate and motivate people to become a better version of themselves. I can look back with an objective view and see that the tests were lessons to build character, as well as valuable tools to apply as I continued to evolve, which is sort of the method to the madness of this whole thing we call life. Some things will never make sense to me logically, but in some cases I learned that I don't have much control. This is how life works. We have to be willing to accept that and adapt, but what we do have control over is how we let things affect who we are. It seems like life has always been trying to teach me something, and in the end it's been up to me to pay attention to the lesson and figure out how I was going to respond.

Having these strokes has given me a chance to discover what my bigger calling in life really is. That has created a fire in my belly and a renewed enthusiasm for life. I could have made choices that might have prevented my strokes, but I have no regrets considering so many positive things have occurred since then. Things happen in our lives whether we like it or not. What's most important is to learn and move forward. For the last 32 years I've spent my life helping people feel better by getting them in shape. It has been a fantastic experience, but now I have a bigger purpose. I want to save lives.

Success is not final, failure is not fatal: it is the courage to continue that counts.

—Winston Churchill

My team and I at my gym Guaranteed Fitness Plus, three years after my strokes. A normal day at the office moving ONWARD and UPWARD

ABOUT THE AUTHOR

Leo Costa, Jr. was born and raised on a family dairy farm in Visalia, California, the oldest of three siblings. His childhood dream was to be a professional athlete. He went on to play sports such as baseball, football, and basketball throughout his school years. He was an All-American baseball player in high school and received a scholarship to play college football. He has always been interested in challenging himself, which lead him to competing in rodeos, becoming a mason, competing in long-distance cycling, becoming a personal trainer, and ultimately his greatest passion, mastering competitive bodybuilding at the world level. He currently owns and operates a personal fitness training studio in Tulare, California. He has owned many studios over the past 32 years, as well as setting up and developing other personal fitness training businesses. He has traveled internationally to give seminars, perform posing exhibitions, promote store openings, and speak at conferences for corporations. In addition to his fitness business, he has developed a supplement line and written many bodybuilding training courses. Leo also has a niche marketing company that he co-owns and has been operating for 20 years that includes self-defense, the art of cigar smoking, fly fishing, and motocross racing. All of his work is geared towards teaching and educating individuals, helping them reach their full potential while striving to be a better version of themselves. Leo believes that his best work lies ahead of him, and he's excited about the possibilities the future holds.

CPSIA information can be obtained
at www.ICGtesting.com
Printed in the USA
FSOW01n0512250716
23078FS